Wakefield Press

Making A Meal Of It

When Rosemary Cadden and Jane Willcox met 25 years ago, Rosemary was impersonating a haggis. Food has been a big part of their relationship ever since.

They later shared their first meal when they found themselves sitting at the same table at a publicity junket while working as journalists for the *Advertiser* newspaper in Adelaide. Although they went in different directions – Rosemary into media relations and Jane to Sydney and into television – they have worked together on projects over the years, including the pilot for a TV series on cooking in Aboriginal communities that never got off the ground.

Jane admits to devouring 'food porn' while Rosemary's passion is 'waste not, want not'. Both appreciate the importance of doing their bit for the planet and reducing their food bills. Most of all they share a love of eating.

MAKING A MEAL OF IT

Smart ways to buy, store and use up food

Jane Willcox and Rosemary Cadden

Wakefield Press

Wakefield Press
1 The Parade West
Kent Town
South Australia 5067
www.wakefieldpress.com.au

First published 2011

Edited by Julia Beaven, Wakefield Press
Designed by Mara Page and Liz Nicholson, designBITE
Cover illustration by Danielle French
Interior illustrations:
Danielle French – avocado, bread, cake, celery, cheese, chicken, egg, meat, rice.
Vallentin Vassileff, istockphotos – asparagus, herbs.
Mariya Stankova, istockphotos – broccoli, pumpkin, mushroom, tomato, zucchini, potatoes, carrot, garlic, capsicum, onion, cabbage, apple, lemon, orange, banana, cauliflower.
Typeset by Clinton Ellicott, Wakefield Press
Printed and bound by Hyde Park Press, Adelaide

National Library of Australia Cataloguing-in-Publication entry

Author:	Cadden, Rosemary.
Title:	Making a meal of it: smart ways to buy, store and use up food / Rosemary Cadden and Jane Willcox.
ISBN:	978 1 86254 913 5 (pbk.).
Subjects:	Food – Storage. Food – Preservation. Food conservation. Cooking.
Other Authors/Contributors:	Willcox, Jane.
Dewey Number:	641.4

Contents

Preface

Two black bananas, one sad carrot, a bunch of slimy coriander and half a loaf of stale bread. That's how this book began; with a quick list of the food about to go to waste in our homes. Talking on the phone one day about how much perfectly good food people throw away, we headed into our respective kitchens to see which of us was the worst waster. Let's just say we called it a draw. And that's when we decided to write this book.

In the months that followed, we got a buzz out of using up food and enjoyed trying out different ideas. We loved the extra money in our pockets and, yes, felt just a little smug about our budding environmental credentials.

We spoke to family and friends; we scoured second-hand bookshops for old-fashioned recipes and researched organisations worldwide that focus on avoiding food waste. We even conducted a survey to find out more about what people discard and how they feel about it.

This book is the best of what we've learnt. Full of tips, ideas and simple recipes, it's a users guide to making the most of the food we feel most guilty about throwing away. How to buy the best, keep it fresh, and make use of every bit – and, when you forget, how to restore and revive. The ideas are simple and flexible, from reinventing leftovers to fast recipes that take advantage of a bulk buy or a garden harvest. You'll not only save time and money but a bit of the planet too.

If you cook, you can use this book. It's for ordinary, busy people, not greenies in mud huts or gourmet cooks with all the latest gadgets. While the TV chefs constantly extol the virtues of using only the freshest produce, we think you can often produce a really tasty meal from odd bits and pieces of less than perfect ingredients.

We wanted to make the book fun to read too, so you'll find lots of useful tips as well as anecdotes and snippets that surprised us, things like:

- Why you shouldn't store zucchinis in the fridge. (And how to tell if they're suffering from it.)
- Turning leftover mashed potato into a strudel cake (and many many more things.)
- Why you shouldn't put a vase of flowers near the fruit bowl.
- Useful things to do with those squeezed orange and lemon cups.

And we answer questions like:

- Which food – not meat, fish or dairy – is the main cause of food poisoning in the home?
- Is it safe to eat the green bits on your potato?
- Why do apes peel their bananas from the other end?
- Which everyday vegetable is healthier cooked than raw?

A study by the Australia Institute estimates that for every five bags of food Australians buy, one is thrown out. The evidence is all too, well, evident: we don't buy sensibly, we don't store properly and we often don't know what to do with what's left over.

And we feel bad about it, too. Our waste survey, through SurveyMonkey, shows nearly 80 per cent of people feel guilty about throwing food away. Fruit and veg topped the list of what our survey participants threw out. Also frequently wasted were fresh herbs, breads, cakes and biscuits.

So what did all this research do to our own wasting habits and what might it do to yours? Well, we're not perfect and we still sometimes ignore our own best advice. But overall, we're definitely throwing out less. We buy more food on special and in bulk because we know we'll use it all up. That means fewer trips to the supermarket. And we deliberately cook extra to create lovely leftover meals. We're more confident about buying different and interesting foods because we've got more than one way to eat them. It's been a ball writing this book and we hope you have just as much fun exploring its pages. So, go on . . .

- Take advantage of that bulk buy special offer.
- Reach to the back of the fridge for that solitary piece of fruit or veg.
- Look again at those bits you cut off and throw out.
- Spend less time shopping for food.
- Reduce the weekly food bill.
- Embrace those leftovers.

The Technical Stuff

We've been arguing for weeks over whether anyone ever reads instructions. Everyone we've spoken to is convinced that we could quote a passage from 'Waltzing Matilda' and no one would give a monkey's! But, if you're honestly interested in the nuts and bolts, or desperately in need of a little sleep . . . read on.

- We have used the term 'sauté with a little oil' – which we know is a tautology, as sauté means fry with a little oil. After much debate, we've erred on the side of the obvious.
- When it comes to baking, size often does matter. But nothing that a bit of extra heat or more time won't fix if you don't want to go out and buy a new model baking tin. This is our excuse for not giving you cooking temperatures and fobbing you off with terms like 'moderate oven'. The little table below reveals all.
- Only the really thrifty – and serial killers – wash and hang out bits of plastic wrap to use again. So we recommend using reusable bags and containers. (Actually, we're lying about the serial killers.)
- We adopt a 'don't ask, don't tell' attitude to salt and pepper. How much you add and what you add it to is your business. However, we felt it worth mentioning for dishes where salt is a vital ingredient.
- We feel pastry is a deeply personal thing too. What you do to create this marvel of modern kitchen architecture in the privacy of your own home is entirely up to you. But we do humbly suggest, if you're using the store-bought stuff, to follow the instructions on the packet.
- Serving sizes, on the other hand, are basic public information – although not always helpful. We both tend to eat more than an average single serving and we hope we're not alone! So how many people our dishes will serve depends on your appetite and how much food you've got to use up. But, as a general rule, most of our suggestions feed four (bird-like) people.

Oven temperatures

Description	Gas		Electric		Mark
	°C	°F	°C	°F	
Very slow	120	250	120	250	½
Slow	150	300	150	300	1–2
Moderately slow	160	325	170	340	3
Moderate	180	350	200	400	4
Moderately hot	190	375	220	425	5–6
Hot	200	400	230	450	6–7
Very hot	230	450	250	475	8–9

Sweet and savoury ideas
to keep the doctor away

Just because apples are popular (second only to bananas) doesn't mean we never waste them. In fact, it's part of the problem. Who hasn't brought home apples from the shop, only to find a couple going soft in the fridge?

Granny's Grannies

Granny Smith was a Sydney grandmother who discovered the new apple variety by accident. In the late 1860s, Maria Ann Smith was running an orchard with her husband in Ryde. One day she threw out the remains of French crab apples, grown in Tasmania. When seedlings sprouted, she decided to nurture them. We now know that the crab apples must have been cross-pollinated with another kind of apple which threw up a completely different, and delicious, variety. Maria showed her neighbours and they took up the tart new fruit and made it famous.

Poor old Granny Smith however died soon after the discovery and never saw how big her new apple was to become.

Buying

Check for crispness by flicking the apple with your fingernail and listening to the sound. The brighter and sharper, the crisper and fresher the apple. If you want to get really picky, the greener the stem usually means the fresher the apple.

One bad apple really can destroy the whole bunch. (This is because apples can contain a lot of the naturally occurring fruit-ripening gas, ethylene.) So, if you're buying in bulk, it's worth investigating the health of the entire bag.

Apples in cold storage are a bit like Walt Disney [there's an urban myth that his cryogenically frozen body lies under Disneyland]. The moment apples are taken out of storage they start 'breathing' again. Trouble is – they taste like a dead man. **Greengrocer**

Season: Look out for the different varieties as they come into season. During the summer, you're probably best buying other fruits.

The different varieties have overlapping seasons. These, in turn, may vary from state to state. Below is a rough guide.

Month and Variety	J	F	M	A	M	J	J	A	S	O	N	D
Jonathan		Picking	Avail	Avail	Avail	Avail	Avail					
Royal Gala		Picking	Avail	Avail	Avail	Avail	Avail	Avail	Avail			
Golden Delicious			Picking	Avail	Avail	Avail	Avail	Avail	Avail	Avail	Avail	Avail
Red Delicious			Picking	Avail	Avail	Avail	Avail	Avail	Avail	Avail	Avail	Avail
Jonagold			Picking	Avail	Avail	Avail	Avail	Avail				
Fuji			Picking	Avail	Avail	Avail	Avail	Avail	Avail	Avail	Avail	Avail
Braeburn				Picking	Avail	Avail	Avail	Avail	Avail	Avail	Avail	Avail
Pink Lady	Avail	Avail		Picking	Avail	Avail	Avail	Avail	Avail	Avail	Avail	Avail
Granny Smith	Avail	Avail	Avail	Picking	Avail	Avail	Avail	Avail	Avail	Avail	Avail	Avail
Jazz				Picking	Avail	Avail						
Sundowner	Avail	Avail			Picking	Avail	Avail	Avail	Avail	Avail	Avail	Avail

Thanks to Apple and Pear Australia for this availability chart.

Storing

Turns out, you can't compare apples with apples. Different varieties have different storage lives. Granny Smith and Fuji, for example, can be stored for three to four weeks in the fridge – twice as long as most other varieties – while Red Delicious are best eaten within a few days of buying. This is because Granny Smith and Fuji give off less ethylene. (It also means that if you're putting an apple in a bag to help ripen another fruit, like an avocado, you'd be better off using another variety.)

Fresh ain't always fresh

Sadly most apples we buy aren't fresh off the tree. Far from it. In 2008, a Sydney newspaper tested a very small sample and found that supermarket apples were up to 10 months old. The secret was out. Apples go straight from the orchard into cold storage. (It was our fault, according to the supermarkets, for wanting the fruit all year round.) The apples were tested by an independent laboratory. Their scientist stated cold storage can keep apples at a good quality for up to six months.

Whole: In the fridge, in a plastic bag with a few holes. This prevents sweating which can lead to mould.

Cut: Keeps better in the fridge. Sprinkling the cut surface with citrus juice, like lemon or orange, stops the apple from going brown without making it sour. It won't last any longer though.

Freezing: Good, if you scald first. Slice, plunge into boiling water then iced water. Pat dry and store in serving sizes. Lasts months but is really only useful for cooked dishes.

Cooked: Apple sauce keeps well for a few days in the fridge. It also freezes for months. Most dishes containing apple freeze well.

WASTE WARRIOR TIP

Someone has peeled the apples. (Not you, naturally.) Now you have a pile of apple peel; perfectly decent food you don't want to chuck in the compost.

Don't panic. Sauté in butter and your fave spices – cinnamon, nutmeg or cloves – and sweeteners – sugar, honey or golden syrup – for a sweet snack.

What can't be improved with sugar and fat?

Using

How much

1 medium apple = 150 grams
= ¾ cup chopped
= ½ cup apple sauce

Try to leave the skin on. It's got two-thirds of the dietary fibre and most of the antioxidants i.e. the good stuff. At the very least, don't bother to peel for apple sauce. If you cook it for long enough, it disappears. Honestly.

Using Up

One Aged Apple

Don't throw out half an apple or even an ageing one. Chop off the bad bits and eat the rest.

- **DESSERT.** Grate and mix through soft ice-cream, rice pudding or custard with a sprinkle of cinnamon.
- **PORRIDGE.** Grate into porridge or over breakfast cereal. Try a sprinkle of cinnamon.
- **SALAD.** Grate into coleslaw, pear and parmesan salad, and any ham-based or smoked fish salads.
- **SALSA.** Chop and add to finely sliced Spanish onion and tomato. Serve with fish.
- **SANDWICH.** Grate onto a ham and seeded-mustard sandwich.
- **SAUCE.** Combine ½ apple, grated, with 4 teaspoons horseradish cream, ¼ cup mayonnaise, 1–2 tablespoons sour cream and ½ teaspoon Dijon mustard. Great with fish, veal and pork. Also spread on hotdogs and sausages.
- **STUFFING.** Add an apple to your onions when preparing stuffing. It goes well with poultry and lamb (see p. 37).
- **ZUCCHINI SLICE.** Apple combines well with zucchini. Replace one of the zucchinis in our slice (see p. 225).

HANDY HINT

Apple adds a subtle sweetness to savoury dishes like casseroles, curries and soups. Chop and add to lamb curry, sausage and bean casserole, and pumpkin soup. There's an apple in the coconut curry (see p. 71) and in the curried soup (see p. 76).

CLOUDY BETTER THAN CLEAR

Dutch researchers have found that cloudy apple juice contains significantly more antioxidants than clear juice. They think this is because of less processing. Of course, you get the most antioxidants out of apples by simply eating them whole!

A Couple of Ageing Apples

- **ASIAN SIDE DISH.** Fry slices in butter with a few drops of sesame oil to team up with Asian-style beef.
- **BAKED.** You can forget how easy and good this is. Core, peel and stuff the cavity with dried fruit, nuts, butter, muesli and sugar or honey. Pour a little water over the apples, cover and bake in a hot oven for 30–40 minutes.
- **CHICKEN SIDE DISH.** Fry slices in butter with chopped thyme or tarragon. Add a splash of white wine and lemon juice. Serve with chicken and pork.
- **COOKED SALAD.** Slice and fry a couple of apples in butter for a few minutes until they colour. Add to ½ shredded cabbage, ½ cup roughly chopped walnuts and ⅓ cup of sultanas. Dress with ½ cup vinegar (apple works well), ⅓ cup oil, 2 tablespoons each honey and mustard. **If you have it:** Add slices of mozzarella and ham.
- **CURRY.** Sauté 1 onion in a little oil, add a couple of crushed cloves of garlic, a 3-centimetre knob grated ginger and 1 tablespoon curry powder. Add 400 g can tomatoes, 2 sliced apples and 400 g can chickpeas. Add sugar to taste. Simmer until apples soften. Serve with a squeeze of lemon and a sprinkle of coriander.
- **SMOOTHIE.** Blend with skin on but core removed. Add milk, ice-cream or yoghurt and a sprinkle of cinnamon.
- **TARTE TARTIN.** If you have a frypan that you can throw in the oven, the rest is easy. Sauté butter and sugar until it starts to colour and caramelise. Fill pan with chunky sliced apples, cook gently until they start to soften. Cool. Cover with a sheet of puff pastry just a bit too big for the pan so you can tuck in the sides. Bake in moderately hot oven for 35 minutes or until pastry is golden. Rest 10 minutes and turn upside down.

Too Many Ageing Apples

- **EASY CHUTNEY.** It gets two ticks. One, you don't have to cook it forever and two, you don't have to sterilise anything. It keeps in the fridge for a week – getting better by the day – and is great with ham and cheese sandwiches. Sauté 2 onions and 2 tablespoons minced ginger in a little oil. Add 6 chopped apples, 1 cup vinegar, 1 cup apple juice and 1–2 teaspoons salt depending on taste. Cook for about 30 minutes or until the liquid is reduced. Makes 3 cups. **Second helpings:** Add 2 cups cooked chicken and throw into a precooked pastry base for chicken and apple pie.

- **APPLE SAUCE.** Core, chop and cook to mush. It's that easy. You can add sugar or lemon juice if you like. Keeps in fridge for a few days and freezes beautifully – or use in the following recipes.

  Biscuits. Combine 1 cup self-raising flour, 1 cup quick oats, ⅓ cup sugar and 1 teaspoon cinnamon. Add 1 cup apple sauce, 2 lightly beaten eggs, 1 cup raisins, 1 cup chopped nuts, ½ cup vegetable oil (mild flavour, not olive) and 1 teaspoon vanilla essence. Roll tablespoons of mixture into balls and flatten with the back of a fork. Bake in moderately hot oven for 8–10 minutes.

  Ham glaze. Combine 1 cup apple sauce with a couple of teaspoons of mustard and ½ cup honey and spread over a leg of ham.

  Mega-easy apple cake. Combine 1 cup cold stewed apples (about 2 apples), 150 grams melted butter (not hot), 1 cup sugar, 2 eggs, 2 cups self-raising flour, 2 teaspoons baking powder, 2 teaspoons cinnamon and 1 teaspoon nutmeg. Stir until well combined. Pour into 30 cm cake tin. Bake in slow oven for 45–60 minutes, maybe longer.

  Sweetener. Instead of sugar, dollop apple sauce into curries and tomato sauces.

EQUIPMENT ALERT

Baking apples? Buy a corer. It's only a few bucks and worth it. Using a knife is a pain in the backside. It can be done but life is too short. Really.

Asparagus

How to stop the rest of the bunch going woody

Asparagus is the crocus of the vegetable world – you know it's spring when Australian asparagus is bountiful in the shops. A guacamole-style dip is just one idea to make the most of it when it's in season and cheap.

WASTE WARRIOR TIP

You don't need to throw the ends away. Slice them up (okay, not the very woody bottom bits) into really thin rounds and you will hardly notice the fibres. Throw the crispy rings into a salad, pop into a stir-fry or save them up and make into soup (see p. 14).

If they're lying down, the tips can bend 60 degrees or more in search of the sun. We don't allow them to do that. But don't worry if this happens at home: bent asparagus tastes just the same as straight! **Arthur G, asparagus farmer**

Buying

A telltale sign of age is the 'ferning out' of the tips. If left in warm conditions they get tough and stringy so pay attention to where and how they're stored in the shop or market: the best method is upright in about a centimetre of water.

Season: Australian asparagus is available from September to April, with the purple variety in the shops around November. The rest of the year, it's likely to come from Peru, the world's biggest asparagus exporter.

Storing

Whole: Asparagus needs cool, humid conditions, so the fridge is best. Wrap it in a damp tea towel or paper towel, pop in a plastic bag and store in the crisper. If you have the space in your fridge, you can stand asparagus upright in one centimetre cold water and cover. It keeps up to a week, especially if you continually change the water.

Freezing: Okay, but it will lose its crunch. Blanch in boiling water for one or two minutes, cool and wrap in airtight bags or containers. Frozen asparagus will keep for eight months. There's no need to defrost before cooking but it's really only for dishes where the asparagus will be essentially mashed.

Colour	Availability	Qualities
Green	98% of market	Can be thin or fat, depending on the age of the whole plant, which lasts about 10 years. It's a misconception that thin means the spears themselves are younger and more tender.
White	1.5% of market	Generally fatter at the base than green or purple. Usually needs to be peeled. In Australia, it's exactly the same variety as the green.
Purple	0.5% of market	Generally wider at the base than green. It's sweeter and fruitier, so good in salads. Acidic dressings (like lemon juice, white wine or vinegar) intensify the colour. Cook too long and it will turn green.

Using

How much

1 bunch asparagus = about 200 grams
1 cup asparagus = 125 grams

The easiest way to get rid of the tough end bits is just to bend each stalk and let it snap where it naturally wants to. Another suggestion is to run a knife along the stalk from the cut end until it meets resistance, cutting at that point. Then there's the mathematical solution: cut them all at around 15 centimetres from the tip.

If you peel the outer layer of thick ones with a vegetable peeler, about two-thirds up from the bottom end, you won't need to cook as long and they're less likely to have stringy bits.

Wait until just before serving to add dressings made with lemon juice or vinegar, otherwise the asparagus will be pickled.

Speedy spears

The Emperor Augustus apparently coined the forgettable proverb 'as quick as cooking asparagus'.

But asparagus does cook very quickly, so it's worth remembering that the spears continue to cook after you take them out of boiling water. Err on the side of undercooked. Tender but crisp is what you're after.

Using Up

A Couple of Stray Spears – Raw

- **BARBECUE.** Drizzle with olive oil and a squeeze of lemon.
- **ROASTED.** Add to your tray of roasted vegetables 10 minutes before the end of cooking time. Sprinkle extra oil if you think it's needed.
- **STIR-FRY.** Throw thin ones in as they come, or slice fat ones into long slivers like green beans. Try them with beef marinated in oyster and sweet chilli sauce, along with mushrooms and spring onions.

A Couple of Stray Spears – Cooked

- **ANTIPASTO.** Wrap strips of prosciutto around spare spears and grill for a few minutes.
- **BREAKFAST.** A spear or two with your boiled egg is a good start to the working day. Or how about with eggs benedict for a Sunday treat.
- **GARNISH.** Sprinkle on bowls of celery or onion soup.
- **PASTA.** Mix with cooked chicken pieces, halved cherry tomatoes, chopped red onion and olives and fold into pasta coated with pesto.
- **SUSHI ROLLS.** Slightly steamed, the spear ends make a good filling with avocado or capsicum.

Half a Bunch

- **ASPARAGUS AND MINT FRITTATA.** Briefly sauté ½–1 bunch steamed and chopped asparagus in a little oil. Add 6 lightly whisked eggs, sprinkle in a small chopped bunch mint and 1½ tablespoons grated parmesan. Cook on low heat until almost set. Top with another 1½ tablespoons grated parmesan. Grill until the cheese is bubbling.

- **ASPARAGUS AND RICOTTA DIP.** Blend 150 grams ricotta cheese, 1 cup steamed asparagus, zest and juice 1 lemon and chilli to taste. Add a little water if you need it.
- **CHICKEN RISOTTO.** Sauté 1 finely chopped onion and 1 crushed clove garlic in butter. Stir in 1 cup risotto rice to coat grains. Add ½ cup white wine and simmer until the liquid disappears. Gradually add 3–4 cups hot chicken stock, 1 bunch chopped asparagus and the zest and juice 2 lemons, boiling gently and stirring occasionally. Cook until almost all the liquid has been absorbed. Stir in 2 cups cooked chicken pieces. Heat through. Stir in ½ cup parmesan and serve.
- **GUACAMOLE.** Use steamed asparagus in place of avocado (see p. 20).
- **SESAME ASPARAGUS.** Toss a handful of asparagus pieces (lightly steamed or cut into thin strips) plus 1 teaspoon each sesame seeds, grated ginger, crushed garlic and finely chopped spring onion in hot sesame oil and stir-fry for a few minutes. Add a few bean sprouts and slices of red capsicum and cook a further minute. Take off the heat and add a dash of soy sauce and a squeeze of lime juice.
- **SMOKED SALMON SALAD.** Combine ½–1 bunch steamed asparagus, 1 apple and 1 pear, cut into thin slices, 2 cups lettuce and 125 grams smoked salmon cut into strips. Toss the lot in a vinaigrette dressing with 1 teaspoon Dijon mustard added. Also works well with crab. **If you have it:** Add ½ cup chopped pecans.
- **VIETNAMESE COLD ROLLS.** Combine lightly steamed asparagus spears with bean sprouts, spring onions and a mixture of herbs such as Thai basil, Vietnamese mint and coriander. Moisten with a little of your chosen dipping sauce just before filling rolls. An easy dipping sauce is equal quantities of sugar, water, fish sauce and lime juice with finely grated garlic and/or a finely sliced chilli.

DID YOU KNOW?

White asparagus is created by depriving it of sunlight, stopping it from producing chlorophyll. But when the white spears are exposed to sunlight, they first turn pink before becoming pale green.

Have a go

Spring Vegetable Soup

Soup is a great way to use up all those asparagus ends you've snapped off. This one is a bit different from the usual creamy versions. For one thing, it's not green! Freezes for up to 2 months.

Ingredients

2–3 teaspoons cooking oil
1 red onion, diced finely
1 red capsicum, diced finely
2 cups asparagus pieces, sliced finely
4 cups vegetable stock
2 tablespoons tomato paste
Salt and pepper to taste
Few drops of Tabasco
Freshly grated parmesan cheese to serve (optional)

Method

Add oil to large saucepan and heat. Add onion, capsicum and asparagus and stir-fry 1 minute.

Add stock and tomato paste and stir well to combine all ingredients.

Bring soup to boil over medium heat, stirring occasionally. Reduce heat and cook gently until vegetables are tender, about 10 minutes.

Remove from heat, season, add Tabasco to taste and serve (sprinkled with parmesan as an option).

Thanks to Australian Asparagus Council for recipe.

Avocado

What to do with that leftover half

Half an avocado in the fridge, turning brown . . . who hasn't had one of those! But hopefully never again. Have you thought of making a curry condiment or soup? Or go Brazilian and turn it into ice-cream.

> **As a teenager, I was handed a teaspoon and half an avocado with some salad dressing in the hole in the middle as my first experience of this exotic food – and it's still my favourite way of eating it.**
>
> **Kate D**

WASTE WARRIOR TIP

Sounds odd, but the best way to get a perfect ripe avocado is to buy a firm, unripe one and ripen it at home. That way you can avoid having to throw away whole sections when you discover the reason it's soft is because it's been bruised by other customers squeezing it.

Buying

Avocados should feel heavy for their size. A ripe one will give slightly when it's gently squeezed. Another way to check for ripeness is to flick its stem, if there is one. If it comes off easily and you can see green underneath, the avocado is getting close to ripe.

Season: Available all year, but most abundant in winter months.

Variety	Availability	Qualities	Size
Hass	Most common (more than 75%)	Pebbly skin Ripe when it's a rich purple colour If it's nearly black it could be overripe	140–340 grams, with a fairly small seed
Shepard	Nearly 20% of the market	Smooth, green skin Flesh doesn't go brown when cut	200–320 grams
Reed	Short season, around November	Round shape Green even when ripe	480–700 grams, with a large seed

Storing

Whole: Before it's ripe, store outside the fridge or the flesh could go mushy and brown. When it's ripe but you don't want it yet, pop your avocado in the fridge to slow down further ripening. It keeps for a few days.

You can speed up the ripening process by putting the avocado in a brown paper bag. It's even faster if you add a banana (even just a banana skin), a ripe apple or a tomato, as they give off the natural ripening gas, ethylene. Store in a warmish spot but away from sunlight.

Cut: To prevent browning, leave the stone in place and squeeze citrus juice or vinegar on the exposed flesh. Wrap avocado closely, expelling all air, and store in the fridge. You've got a couple of days before the surface starts to brown.

Pureed: Push plastic wrap onto the surface of guacamole, dip or pureed avocado, making sure there's no air. Store in the fridge.

Freezing: Yes, you can freeze avocado. Simply remove the skin and seed, cut into quarters and store in an airtight container for up to two months.

Frozen pureed avocado should last for three to six months in an airtight container. You can add a tablespoon of lemon juice for every two avocados to prevent browning. Use for guacamole, dips and spreads.

DID YOU KNOW?

If you have an avocado tree, that's the best place to store them. There's something in the leaves that prevents ripening and they're happy for seven months or more.

Using

How much

1 medium avocado = 250 grams
= ⅔ cup puree

Avocado shells can be used as serving dishes.

For hot dishes like pasta and pizza, it's best to add the avocado just before serving.

MYTHBUSTER

There's no truth in the myth that putting the avocado seed back in a dip will prevent browning.

Doubly delightful

Adding avocado to your salad can make it healthier. Research has shown that avocados may help you to absorb more nutrients from the other salad ingredients. These include lycopene and betacarotene found in tomatoes and leafy green vegetables.

Using Up

A Sad Half

- **SCRAMBLED EGGS.** Add avocado, thinly sliced red onion and some dill for a Sunday special.
- **BABY FOOD.** Mash avocado on its own or with some banana.
- **CHICKEN AND CORN SOUP.** Likes a diced avocado garnish on top. So too does tomato soup.
- **MASH.** Mash with potato and sprinkle with paprika to serve with meat.
- **PASTA SAUCE.** Add chopped-up avocado to tomato-based pasta sauce just before serving. Or add thin slices of avocado before the final layer of meat sauce and cheese in lasagne.
- **PIZZA TOPPING.** Try avocado slivers with cooked chicken, halved cherry tomatoes, chopped spring onion and a sprinkling of fetta cheese.
- **RELISH.** Mash avocado into prepared relish to make it go further. Helps to take the bite out of a particularly spicy one too.
- **SPREAD.** Replace butter or mayonnaise on sandwiches. Dab toast with Vegemite and spread with avocado. Spread over chicken burger.
- **TAHINI SAUCE.** Mix together ½ an avocado, 2 tablespoons tahini and 1 tablespoon yoghurt. Add a little water if necessary. Pour over cauliflower or broccoli.
- **TOFU DIP.** Puree equal amounts of avocado and silken tofu. (Squeeze as much moisture as possible out of tofu beforehand.) Season with Tabasco and lemon juice.

A Firm Happy Half

- **ASIAN BROCCOLINI.** Combine ½ tablespoon each crushed garlic and grated ginger and some finely chopped chilli. Add equal quantity of sesame oil and kecap manis. Toss broccolini in sauce until coated and stir-fry, using up any leftover sauce. Toss in slices of avocado at the end along with toasted sesame seeds.
- **AVOCADO HALVES.** That hole in the middle is just begging to be filled. Drip in some olive oil and balsamic vinegar or soy sauce. Or try these:

  Crumbled bacon and scrambled egg.

  A couple of prawns in curried mayonnaise.

  Prawns, pitted olives and celery drizzled with salad dressing.
- **AVOCADO WRAPS.** You like prosciutto wrapped around melon wedges? Try firm avocado wedges for a change. Or both together.
- **SALAD.** Goes in just about any combination. Try with spinach, orange slices and pine nuts.

Sweet cool avocado

Ice blocks. Blend avocado and banana with a little honey. Freeze in iceblock holders.

Ice-cream. Blend together 2 avocados and ¼ honeydew melon with the juice 1 lemon, ½ cup natural yoghurt and sugar to taste. Whip 2 eggwhites until peaks form and fold into mixture. Freeze for at least 6 hours.

Shake. Blend together ½ avocado, 1 tablespoon honey, juice 1 lemon, juice 1 orange and fresh mint. Filipinos puree avocados with sugar and milk for a dessert drink.

An Overripe Whole

- **ASIAN DRESSING.** Blend 1 tablespoon soy sauce, 1 teaspoon honey and 1 avocado. Mix in 1 red onion, ½ cup coriander and 1 tomato, all finely chopped. Serve over chicken or prawns.

- **CHEESECAKE.** Avocado makes an extra creamy cheesecake that's worth trying for the light green colour alone. Make a biscuit base (see p. 51). Blend 500 grams cream cheese (low-fat works well as the avocado is rich) with 2 avocados and 1 cup honey until smooth. Add 3 eggs, 1 teaspoon vanilla essence, ½ teaspoon cinnamon and zest 1 lime. Blend until creamy. Pour mixture into prepared 20 cm loose-bottomed cake tin and bake in a moderately slow oven for about 1 hour. It will still feel a little soft to the touch, but will firm up as it cools. Allow to cool in oven then put in the fridge. **If you have it:** Spread top with whipped cream and garnish with kiwi fruit.

- **COLD SOUP.** Blend 1 avocado, 200 g tub plain yoghurt, 1 cup vegetable stock, dash of lime juice, a few tablespoons of chopped chives. Add 1 cup either chopped cucumbers or diced tomatoes. Chill and serve. **If you have it:** Add 1 tablespoon Dijon mustard, or a handful of chopped dill.

- **CURRY SAUCE.** Makes a meal of steamed vegies. Blend together 1 avocado with 1 cup orange juice, 1 teaspoon curry powder and a handful of fresh herbs. Try parsley, coriander or basil.

- **GUACAMOLE.** Some like it pureed, some like it chunky. A basic recipe is 1 avocado, 2 tablespoons finely chopped onion, 1 small ripe chopped tomato, 1 crushed clove garlic, a handful of chopped coriander, chilli to taste and the juice 1 lime or lemon.

- **HOT SOUP.** Blend avocado with sour cream and lime juice to taste. Slowly add to simmering chicken stock – but be careful not to let it get too hot to avoid the mixture curdling. Serve immediately.

Have a go

Avocado Mousse with Smoked Salmon

A luxurious mousse without the hassle of gelatine or eggwhites.

Ingredients

2 avocados
100 g cream cheese
1 teaspoon wasabi paste
½ bunch dill or tarragon, chopped
Salt and pepper to taste
1 tablespoons lime juice
200 g sliced smoked salmon

Method

Mix avocado flesh, cream cheese, wasabi paste and herbs with a fork until quite smooth.

Gradually add lime juice until desired taste. Make sure mixture remains quite firm.

Season and then chill in fridge for at least 30 minutes.

Roll up a little of the mixture in each smoked salmon slice.

Banana

Heaven on a stick and other secrets

They're one of nature's greatest self-wrapped snack foods, but the downside is that when bananas start to ripen, it's a speedy process to mushy pulp. If you've been throwing out those speckled and brown bananas, we have some great ideas for you. However, it's not compulsory to wait until those bananas are overripe before you cook them!

Bananas, stuck onto paddle pop sticks, rolled in chocolate and then rolled in rice bubbles and frozen. That's what I remember from summer school holidays as a kid. Yum. **Mike D**

Who's the smart one?

Have a look next time you're at the zoo and see how the apes eat bananas. They peel theirs from the opposite end to us. Try it and you'll find you're less likely to get the stringy bits. Who's the smart one then . . .

Buying

Bananas keep ripening after they're picked. They're considered at their peak when a few speckles appear on the bright yellow skins – but it's a matter of personal taste.

Bananas that look dull have probably become too cold in storage. They won't ripen very well, so they'll never have a decent flavour.

Lady Finger and **Gold Finger** are good for fresh fruit salads. The flesh holds its colour better and doesn't darken as quickly as other varieties when cut.

Eco bananas (the ones with the waxed tips) aren't organic, but that coloured tip does mean they come from farms that are committed to cutting back on synthetic fertilisers and insecticides. The wax is biodegradable.

Season: Available all year round.

Storing

Whole: Best kept at room temperature.

If you want to speed up the ripening process, put them in a paper bag at room temperature – add a ripe apple for an even quicker result.

On the other hand, if they've ripened before you want to eat them, bananas can be stored in the fridge for a couple of days to make them last a little bit longer. The skins get dark but it doesn't affect the taste. However, if you find the colour change off-putting, wrap them individually in newspaper or foil to slow down the process.

Keep your bananas away from other fruit as they give off massive doses of the natural ripening gas – ethylene.

Cut: To stop browning, dip in lemon juice or other citrus fruit.

Freezing: Great. Stick them in the freezer, skin and all. You can also peel, then wrap tightly before freezing; or go one step further and blend into a puree first.

Banana leaves

There's a theory that the fruit of the Tree of Knowledge in the Garden of Eden was actually a banana. While Adam and Eve may have used banana leaves for clothing, we use them to wrap up dishes. Such a lovely alternative to aluminum foil. And then you can use them as serving plates.

Buy banana leaves fresh or frozen from Asian stores. Cut the leaves to size with scissors. Leftover leaves can be stored in a plastic bag in the freezer.

WASTE WARRIOR TIP

Banana skins are full of potassium. Mince them up and feed to your indoor plants, especially ferns, and watch them thrive. Or just throw whole banana skins under your rose bushes.

Using

How much

1 medium banana = ⅓–½ cup mashed
= 80 grams peeled

Using Up

One Speckled Freckled Specimen

- **BACON.** Wrap banana pieces in bacon, secure with a toothpick and grill. **If you have it:** Slice banana pieces lengthwise, spread with a mixture of cream cheese and chopped parsley and reunite the halves before wrapping in bacon.
- **CHICKEN.** Slice chicken breast in two like a book, lay half a banana, cut lengthwise, at the fold and wrap the chicken around it. Fry for a few minutes on both sides and then pop in moderate oven for 10–15 minutes, or do the lot in the frypan. Go completely bananas and make a sauce to pour over the chicken breast. Simmer ½ cup each cream and chicken stock, letting it reduce by about one third, and then add some finely chopped banana and dill.
- **GREEK-STYLE DESSERT.** Combine 1 banana cut into thick slices, juice ½ a lemon and 5 cardamom seeds (crush the pods to get to the seeds). Drizzle honey over the mixture and serve with Greek yoghurt.
- **INDIAN SIDE DISH.** Coat slices with a squeeze of lemon juice and desiccated coconut as an accompaniment for an Indian meal.
- **MUESLI.** If that last banana is getting too soft to eat fresh, try cooking it instead. Slice and heat with a little butter and brown sugar and add to your muesli with some extra nuts and dried fruit.

Handy hint

Banana loves curry, so it's a different way to use up an ageing one.

Vegie or lentil curry. Chop and pop banana slices into the mix for a subtle fruity flavour. The older the banana, the stronger the flavour.

Curried and crumbed. Cut banana in two, lengthwise. Coat with mixture of ¼ breadcrumbs, a couple of teaspoons of curry powder and a splash of soy sauce. Fry, grill or put on the barbie. Tastes good with fish.

Chicken schnitzel. Mash and spread on chicken breast before crumbing.

If you have more than one banana, check out the banana curry sauce (see p. 28).

- **PANCAKES.** Mash up and add to your pancake mix. If they're still decent enough for public display, just slice onto cooked pancakes and fold.
- **TOASTED SANDWICH.** Elvis loved this concoction: banana, bacon, peanut butter and/or honey. Warning: do not eat in Elvis-like quantities.
- **WONTONS.** For a fruity variation, use a slice of banana as the filling for each tasty little dumpling. One banana will make about 20. Lightly brush wrappers along the edges with cold water. Scrunch up into a pouch, squeezing to seal the edges together. Do not overfill. Fry for 2–3 minutes until golden or steam for about 15–20 minutes, making sure wontons don't touch each other. (A tip is to line steamer with non-stick baking paper with slits in it.) Drizzle with honey and sprinkle with toasted sesame seeds.

FLOWERING FACT

Do your flowers a favour and put the vase in another room from the fruit bowl, particularly your bananas. It's the ethylene gas from the fruit that makes those petals feel poorly.

A Speckled Handful

- **ASPARAGUS SALAD.** Add 2–3 sliced bananas to a couple of bunches of steamed asparagus and 2 tomatoes cut into wedges. Dress with 2 tablespoons wine vinegar, ½ cup olive oil, 2 teaspoons lemon juice and 2 teaspoons Dijon mustard.
- **BOOZY BANANA BREAD-AND-BUTTER PUDDING.** A great way to use 3 or 4 overripe bananas. Just add them (sliced or mashed) to the basic bread and butter pudding recipe (see p. 35). The boozy bit is the sauce. Gently heat ½ cup butter, 1 cup brown sugar, a good splash of your favourite liqueur and a pinch of nutmeg until the sugar dissolves. Whisk an egg until frothy and then whisk into the sauce. Bring the mixture to a simmer, whisking until thickened. Cool and pour over each serve.

WHIPPED CREAM

Add finely sliced banana to eggwhites and beat until stiff as a substitute for whipped cream.

- **CHEESECAKE.** Blend 2 ripe bananas with the cream cheese mixture in your favourite baked cheesecake recipe. Or just put a layer of banana slices on the biscuit base. Shredded coconut and cream go well over the top.
- **CLASSIC BANANA AND CARAMEL PIE.** This retro pie recipe has been reinvented over the years under various nom de plumes. Probably because it's hard to go past the combination of banana and caramel. For the caramel, heat together ⅓ cup butter and ⅓ cup caster sugar until sugar dissolves. Add 390 g can condensed milk and slowly bring to the boil, stirring continuously. As soon as the mixture thickens, remove from the heat and allow to cool. Pour into biscuit base (see p. 51). Arrange 2 sliced bananas over caramel and top with whipped cream. **If you have it:** Sprinkle with shaved chocolate.
- **CURRIED SAUCE.** For seafood or chicken. Sauté 1 diced onion, some chopped celery and 1 crushed clove garlic in a little oil for about 3 minutes. Add 1 tablespoon curry powder, ½ teaspoon grated ginger, ½ teaspoon cardamom, pinch of cinnamon and ground nutmeg and ½ teaspoon white pepper. Sauté for another minute. Add 4 sliced bananas and 2 cups chicken stock. Simmer for 20 minutes. Add more stock to thin if necessary. Puree.

- **FRITTERS.** Combine 3 mashed bananas and 3 tablespoons sugar. Gradually stir in 1 cup plain flour with a little milk to make a batter that's halfway between sloppy and stiff. Fry heaped tablespoonfuls each side until golden. Sprinkle with caster sugar.
- **FRUIT PIZZA.** No matter whether you're a lover or hater of pineapple on your savoury pizza, you'll love this totally fruity version. Prepare or buy a biscuit dough for the base. Bake it for about 10 minutes until lightly brown. Cool. Blend ½ cup sugar with 250 grams cream cheese and spread over base. Arrange banana slices and any other fruit you want on top. Strawberries add colour. Sprinkle banana slices with lemon to stop them from browning. **If you have it:** Pour chocolate sauce over just before serving.
- **ORANGE SAUCE.** For pork. Heat 1 cup orange juice, zest 1 orange and 2 tablespoons brown sugar until sugar dissolves. Add 3 sliced bananas and cook until soft. Cool sauce and pour over meat.
- **RAITA.** Chop 2 bananas into bite-sized pieces and sprinkle with lemon juice. Add 250 g tub plain yoghurt, ½ teaspoon each ground cumin and chilli powder, ¼ cup raisins and a good pinch of salt. Cover and chill for 1 hour. Serve sprinkled with black pepper or paprika.
- **SWEET POTATO AND BANANA CRUMBLE.** This is a simple version of a dish enjoyed in the Deep South of the US of A. Roast 2 large sweet potatoes (scrubbed) for 30 minutes in a moderately hot oven and add 4 bananas (unpeeled) for another 15 minutes, until all are very soft. When cool, scoop out potato flesh and peel bananas. Beat together with ½ cup butter, ¼ cup honey and pinch of salt until fluffy. Spoon into baking dish. For the crumble, rub together ½ cup plain flour, ½ cup butter, ¾ cup brown sugar and 1½ cups chopped pecans until the mixture is the consistency of coarse crumbs. Sprinkle over the sweet potatoes. Bake for about 20 minutes, until the crumbs are golden. Serve hot.

Have a go

Banana Strudel

Not as well known as the traditional German apple strudel, German bananas being a scarce commodity.

Ingredients

2 ripe bananas, sliced
1 tablespoon orange juice
4 sheets filo pastry
3 tablespoons butter
1 tablespoon desiccated coconut
¼ cup sultanas
¼ cup pecans, chopped
¾ teaspoon cinnamon
1 tablespoon honey
½ tablespoon caster sugar

Method

Soak banana slices in orange juice.

Brush each sheet of filo pastry with melted butter and place on top of each other.

Drain bananas and combine with desiccated coconut, sultanas, pecans, ½ teaspoon ground cinnamon and honey.

Spread the filling at one end of the filo square, covering about a third and leaving a 5 centimetre space along both sides.

Roll pastry over the mixture and continue rolling, tucking in each end to create a seal, until you have a tight filo parcel log. Brush the top with butter.

Combine remaining cinnamon with caster sugar and sprinkle over strudel.

Cut some steam vents diagonally along top of strudel.

Bake in a moderate oven for about 20 minutes or until golden brown and crispy on the base. Serve in slices with cream and/or vanilla ice-cream. **If you have it:** Replace coconut, sultanas and cinnamon with 60 grams grated chocolate.

Bread

Got a freezer full of icy bread?
There are yummier ways to go

Got a freezer full of icy bread? There are more interesting ways to go than toasting. And there's only so much bread those ducks can handle! We've turned to smart peasant food and anything-but-dull Depression dinners for solutions.

> **I used to buy fancy artisan loaves that turned to stone before I used them up. Now I buy rolls and slice them.** **Ana N**

WASTE WARRIOR TIP

To revive a loaf of stale bread, dip it in cold water and bake in a moderate oven for 10 minutes or so. And soft crackers get a new crisp lease of life if you dry them out for 5 minutes in a moderate oven just before serving.

Note: These tricks only work once!

Buying

Loaves with an open crumb are great for soaking up sauces and serving with soup. Bread for bruschetta and open sandwiches needs a firmer crumb. As a rule, the more open the crumb, the quicker the bread will dry out. So high tops, which expand during baking, will dry out quicker than sandwich loaves, which have been compressed a bit.

French sticks and baguettes with low fat and low sugar content keep fresh for a day, sourdough for two or three, and rye for up to five days.

> **I love sourdough bread when it's fresh. It's just as nice a day or two later. And then it makes yummy bread salad later in the week.** **Jane W**

Storing

The bread bin may not be the fixture it once was in the kitchen, but it's probably still the best place to store your rolls and loaves. Fridge temperatures dry out bread products. However, moist breads go mouldy so a bit of drying out might not be such a bad thing.

It's best to keep your bread in the wrapping you bought it in. This is usually a plastic bag for store-bought and sliced bread and paper bags for artisan-style bread. The idea is that the paper bag keeps the crust crusty. If you've noticed the crust on crusty bread getting tougher after a couple of days, you're perfectly correct. That's what happens when air gets to it.

Cut: Keep the 'ender' as a lid on the end of your loaf to help keep it fresh.

Soft breadcrumbs: Best to make as you need as they quickly go mouldy. For small quantities, the easiest solution is to grate a piece of bread straight from the freezer.

Freezing: You can freeze bread in all its forms – whole or sliced, rolls and breadcrumbs. Wrap bread really well to make sure it's airtight to avoid that 'frostbitten' taste. Use a non-porous bag. The plastic bag they're sold in is the best because freezer bags are slightly porous. You can also wrap tightly in foil.

Bread lasts for up to three months, though the crusts on crusty loaves will start to flake after a week or so.

Cool sandwiches

You can prepare and freeze an entire week's supply of sandwiches for lunches in one go. Good fillings include peanut butter, cheese and sliced meat. Avoid hard-boiled eggs: the whites go hard. Put moist ingredients like tomato sauce and mustard between meat and cheese slices to stop the bread going soggy. Wrap each sandwich separately and put in plastic sandwich bag, then a freezer bag.

Pop in the lunch box and they thaw out – still in the wrapper – just in time for lunch.

Thawing

For rolls and loaves, just remove wrapping and thaw at room temperature. To bring back the crustiness, pop into a moderate oven, about 15 minutes for rolls and small loaves and 30 minutes for large loaves. But it's only nice if you eat it straight away and you can only do it once. Protect soft crusts with a loose piece of foil but leave crusty bread uncovered.

Frozen slices can be toasted without thawing.

Using the microwave for bread is a black art. Some have reported success, but we produced either soggy or rubbery results. Experiment if you dare.

Using

Easy slicing

To tackle that fresh loaf try:

- Dipping the knife into boiling water first.
- Chilling the bread in the fridge before slicing.

And think about saving the breadcrumbs. Any seeds (sunflower etc.) that fall off the crust can be added to a salad.

Using Up

Loaves, Rolls and Odd Slices

- **ALMOND SKORDALIA.** Pour ½ cup warm milk over 2 slices of bread (minus crusts) and stand for 5 minutes. Blend bread, ½ cup flaked almonds, 1 large clove garlic and juice and zest 1 lemon. Slowly add olive oil – up to 5 tablespoons. If mixture is still too stiff, add a little water. Good with lamb and fish. See p. 193 for a garlicky potato version.

- **BREAD AND BUTTER PUDDING.** The original, made with stale bread and water in times of hardship, has come a long way. The basic recipe is 6 slices of buttered bread, a handful of raisins or sultanas and 2 tablespoons sugar layered in a dish. Pour over a mixture of 3 beaten eggs and 2 cups milk and leave for 15–30 minutes before baking in a slow to moderate oven for 45 minutes or so. Spreading jam on the bread is an easy way to add a fruity flavour. Croissants or brioche bread turn it into a dinner-party dessert. See p. 50 and p. 202 for other ideas.

- **CROUTONS.** Cubes of old bread crisped in the oven are great in pea, bean and creamed soups, gazpacho and in salads. Butter the cubes if you like before baking, or fry the pieces in a little olive oil, adding parmesan for that extra touch. Use plain ones for cheese fondue.

- **CRUMBLE.** Stretch your sweet crumble topping by adding a cup of soft breadcrumbs.

- **DUMPLINGS.** These are a lighter alternative to traditional flour dumplings. Make small ones to pop in your soup. Tear half a loaf into pieces and soak in ½ cup milk. Sauté 1 chopped onion in a little oil and add to bread mixture with 2 eggs, 1 tablespoon flour and some of your favourite herbs. Make firm balls and drop in boiling water. Lower the heat and simmer for 20 minutes. They're cooked when they rise to the surface and spin.

- **EMPAREDADOS CALIENTES.** A Latin American version of croque monsieur – French bread to you and me. The basic idea is slapping a slice of ham (and cheese if you have it) between two slices of stale bread dipped in an egg and milk mixture then fry.

- **ITALIAN TOMATO SALAD.** Day-old bread is one of the main ingredients in Italian panzanella. Tear about 4 slices into pieces (sourdough is great) and fry in olive oil until golden. Toss them with 4–5 very ripe, chopped tomatoes, 1 small finely sliced red onion, and a handful of shredded basil. Drizzle over a dressing of ½ cup olive oil, 1 crushed clove garlic and 2 tablespoons red vinegar, and let it stand for 30 minutes. **If you have it:** Sauté some chopped bacon with the onion.

- **MUFFIN BASES.** Press bread slices into patty tins, buttered side down. Bake in a moderate oven for 10 minutes. Fill with mixture of 4 lightly beaten eggs, 2 tablespoons milk and ½ cup grated cheese. Top with a tomato slice. Bake in a moderate oven until bubbling. **If you have it:** Scoop the inside out of rolls as mock vol-au-vent cases. Use the scooped out bread in the filling – or turn into breadcrumbs.

HANDY HINT

Use stale bread to thicken sauces and stews. Just rip into chunks and it will dissolve on cooking. Even better, if it's one of those specialty flavoured breads – like olive and parmesan – it adds extra flavour to the dish.

Add to meatball and meatloaf mixture. Soak in milk, squeeze out the moisture and add to your minced pork, lamb or beef for a lighter, looser texture.

- **QUEEN OF PUDDINGS.** This is bread pudding taken to royal levels. Heat 1¼ cups milk and beat in 2 egg yolks. Add 4 slices of bread cut into small pieces, grated rind 1 lemon and 1½ tablespoons sugar. Bake in moderately slow oven for 45 minutes. Spread some jam on the pudding and top with meringue, made by whisking the 2 eggwhites until stiff and folding in ¼ cup caster sugar. Pop back into a moderate oven for 15 minutes until the meringue turns golden and crisp.

- **SALSA VERDE.** Soak 2 big slices of bread in a little milk to soften. Blend with 1 clove garlic, 4–5 anchovies, ½ cup olive oil and 1 cup chopped parsley. Dollop on boiled potatoes, team with chicken, serve with the backyard barbie, or call it a dip and serve with carrot and celery sticks.

- **SAVOURY ROLY-POLY.** Cut crusts off slices and roll thin. Spray with oil, sprinkle with cheese, roll up, sprinkle with seeds (sesame, poppy or nigella) and secure with toothpicks. Bake in moderate oven for 15 minutes.

- **SOUP.** Italian ribolleta (which means reboiled) transforms a bean-tomato style soup on its second day. Options are to put bits of bread in the bottom of the soup bowl before pouring soup over it; stick the bread in the soup pot while it's bubbling; or line a baking dish with day-old bread, pour over the soup and bake.
- **STUFFING.** Make crumbs with day-old bread minus the crusts in the food processor – or just break the bread into pieces to give a quicker but lumpier result. Doesn't have to be stuffed inside anything either. For baking alongside or inside chicken, sauté some herbs and finely chopped onion in butter, add soft breadcrumbs or pieces and bind together with stock.
- **SUMMER CAKE.** Simmer 2 thinly sliced apples and 6 cups soft fruit (like berries) for about 10 minutes in syrup made with 1 cup water and 2 tablespoons sugar. Pour off the juice and save for later and puree the fruit. Taste and add sugar if needed. Completely cover the bottom of a flat dish with thin slices of bread. Cover with some puree to soak the bread. Continue alternating layers of bread with layers of puree until all the puree is used up. Finish with a bread layer. Pour over the saved juice. Press the cake down with a plate plus something heavy on top from your pantry. Leave overnight. Serve with cream.

HANDY HINT

Fluffy packaged white bread tends to disappear when offered a second life as a pudding, while the crusts of crisp baguettes and artisan breads never really soften.

Breadcrumbs

How much

1 slice bread = ½ cup breadcrumbs

No amount of nagging stops some family members from cutting off the bread crusts. So stop nagging and collect crusts in the freezer. When you have a bagful, break them down to the size you want for coating rissoles etc. You can use a food processor or grate while the bread is still frozen.

For a crisper coating, put all those crusts, loaf ends and stale bits in the bottom of a slow oven until they're really dry. Put through the processor or bash with a rolling pin. This is also a solution for making breadcrumbs more easily from fresh bread.

For seasoned breadcrumbs, just add dried or fresh herbs before storing (see Hint No 2 p. 121). Or fry crumbs lightly in butter and herbs until golden brown, drain them well on kitchen paper, and leave in a cool place to dry out before storing. These homemade browned breadcrumbs can be stored in an airtight jar, in a dry place, for up to a month. Or stick in the freezer for at least 2–3 months.

WASTE WARRIOR TIP

Keep a jar for breadcrumb mix; the crumbs from slicing a fresh loaf, all those broken or stale savoury biscuits and crackers, even those crumbs at the bottom of the biscuit barrel or cereal carton.

- **BREAD SAUCE.** This ancient sauce is a Christmas staple in the northern hemisphere and it works just as well with Aussie fare of chook and snags. The trick is to allow plenty of time for the flavours to soak into the milk. Heat a thinly sliced onion, 2–4 cloves and a bay leaf in 1 cup milk for about 10 minutes. Strain and add ⅔ cup soft breadcrumbs. Cook slowly without boiling until crumbs swell. Mix in 2 tablespoons butter and season. Serve hot. **If you have it:** Swap the bay leaf for some other herbs you have handy.
- **CAULIFLOWER.** Lightly fry a cup of breadcrumbs along with pine nuts or almond slivers in melted butter. Sprinkle over cauliflower and top with grated parmesan.
- **GAZPACHO.** A cup of breadcrumbs adds bulk and texture to this tasty cold soup (see p. 218).
- **MACARONI AND CHEESE.** Add 1 cup soft breadcrumbs to the sauce to make your macaroni go further. Makes the dish a bit lighter too.
- **SAVOURY CRUMBLE.** To every cup of herby breadcrumbs add ¼ cup grated parmesan. Sprinkle over casseroles and cooked pasta and vegetable dishes. Bake until golden.
- **SCHNITZELS.** For crumbed dishes like schnitzels, crumbed fish and croquettes, coat first in beaten egg, then flour, then breadcrumbs.
- **STUFFED CAPSICUM.** Combine 1 cup soft breadcrumbs with 4 tablespoons shaved parmesan, 3 chopped anchovies, ½ cup flat leaf parsley, 2 crushed cloves garlic, 1 teaspoon thyme and a little oil. Slice the tops off 2 capsicums. Carefully remove membrane and seeds and fill with stuffing. Replace tops, brush over the lot with oil and bake in a moderate oven for 35–40 minutes. **If you have it:** Add 1½ tablespoons capers and/or ⅓ cup sliced olives.

Flat Bread

- **LEBANESE SALAD (FATTOUSH).** Toast day-old pita rounds in the oven until crisp and light brown (about 10 minutes). Break into bite-sized pieces and add to a salad of chopped ripe tomatoes, sliced cucumber, chopped spring onions, mint and parsley. Add a dressing of ½ cup olive oil, ½ cup lemon juice, 1 crushed clove garlic, 1 teaspoon Dijon mustard and chilli. For the non purists, you can replace lemon juice with ¼ cup white balsamic vinegar.
- **PIZZA BASE.** Use stale pita or pocket bread rounds. Spread with homemade tomato sauce. Top with a mixture of olives, roasted capsicum slices, prosciutto and basil leaves. Sprinkle with fetta cheese and warm through in oven.
- **QUICHE BASE.** Liberally butter flat bread and use instead of pastry.
- **SWEET SNACK.** Spread honey, then mashed banana over a stale pita round, top with desiccated coconut and heat under the griller.

FRITTER SOLUTION

If you are collecting rather a lot of breadcrumbs and looking for an outlet – try replacing flour in fritter recipes with breadcrumbs.

Broccoli

How to use every morsel

Broccoli tends to polarise people. For those of us who love broccoli, it's probably more versatile than you think. For the rest, we have a few tricks up our sleeve to help create converts.

Don't assume your kids hate broccoli. Mine love it. We call them 'trees' and count how many we eat. **Mum**

WASTE WARRIOR TIP

Don't throw away the stems. Chop and use just like the florets. The stems are lovely when eaten raw as a crunchy snack and have a milder flavour than the rest of the broccoli. You may need to peel the very end of the stem, it can be stringy.

Buying

Intense colours likely mean high nutritional content, even some purple colouring is fine. It was probably caused by frost and disappears on cooking.

Blooming yellow flowers are a sign that the broccoli is old. (But not a problem with broccolini.)

Splits or cracks on the bottom of the stem aren't necessarily a bad sign and may have been caused by a growth spurt.

Season: Best around the winter months, April to November.

Broccolini

It looks like baby broccoli but it's not. Broccolini is actually a cross between broccoli and Chinese kale. Developed in Japan, it can be substituted for broccoli in recipes, or vice versa. Broccolini acts a bit like a baby vegie though. It's more delicate and doesn't keep as long as broccoli because the stems are thinner.

Storing

Whole: In a plastic bag in the fridge with a sprinkle of water. You probably won't need to add any, just don't wipe off any water from the supermarket or vegetable shop. Broccoli keeps for up to a week.

Cut: Treat like the whole broccoli, in a sealed container in the fridge. The smaller the broccoli piece the shorter the lifespan.

Freezing: Great, cut head into florets and stem into bite-sized pieces, cook for three minutes then cool and freeze. Keeps for months.

Cooked: Put leftover cooked broccoli in tightly covered container and store in the refrigerator for a few days.

HEAVY BREATHER

Broccoli has the highest respiration rate of any fruit or vegetable. So while they all breathe, broccoli pants! This means it dries out fast because it loses moisture at the same time. Farmers even suggest that if you leave your broccoli in the car on a hot day, it will start to go soft very quickly. (But they don't like you leaving any of their precious produce in such a warm place.)

Getting the good stuff

Broccoli is particularly prone to losing its nutrients. To make sure you get as much Vitamin C, betacarotene, folate, iron and calcium as you can:

- Eat as soon as you can after buying.
- Cook as little as possible, i.e. keep it a bit crunchy.
- Cook in as little water as possible, e.g. steam rather than boil.

Using

How much

1 medium broccoli = 200–300 grams
= 2–3 cups
5 broccoli florets = 1 cup

In most recipes broccoli and cauliflower may be substituted for one another, so check cauliflower chapter too.

Using Up

A Few Floppy Florets (and stem)

- **EGG/POTATO SALAD.** Lightly steam and add to salads. Try hard-boiled eggs, olives and sliced red onion. Bulk it out with steamed potato. Use a creamy dressing. Mayonnaise with chopped tarragon is perfect.
- **FRITTERS.** Makes great fritters, especially when combined with cooked cauliflower, potato, peas and carrot (see p. 72).
- **LASAGNE, QUICHE OR FRITTATA.** Chop and throw it into the mix for a colourful addition to any pasta or egg dish.
- **SOUP.** Puree cooked broccoli, cauliflower, apple (or apple sauce) and potato with chicken stock and serve with yoghurt, sour cream or cream. Serve hot, sprinkled with chopped chives, basil or tarragon.
- **STIR-FRY/COCONUT MILK CURRIES.** Broccoli can be added to most stir-fries as well as red and green Thai curries and creamy coconut dishes.
- **VEGETABLE BAKE.** Dig out whatever else may be lurking in the crisper, like cauliflower, potato, pumpkin or carrots. Chop into smallish pieces. Pan-fry for a few minutes with a couple of cloves of garlic. Tip into ovenproof dish, pour over two lightly beaten eggs mixed with ½ cup milk. Sprinkle generously with grated cheese and bake until just soft.

A Floppy Forgotten Head

- **ANCHOVIES.** Pan-fry 3–4 crushed cloves garlic, chilli to taste and 4 chopped anchovies. Add chopped broccoli and a few tablespoons of stock or water. Cover and steam until broccoli is cooked. Serve as side dish or toss through pasta, topped with parmesan.
- **CHICKEN.** Pan-fry 4 chicken breasts, cut into strips, until browned. Add 2 cloves garlic, a 2-centimetre knob ginger (optional) and broccoli pieces with a few tablespoons of stock

or water. Heat until chicken and broccoli are cooked. **If you have it:** Add ⅓ cup chopped almonds and ½ cup chopped basil.

- **CHORIZO RISOTTO.** Pan-fry 1–2 sliced chorizo. Stir in 1½ cups risotto rice to coat grains. Extra oil or butter shouldn't be needed, there's enough in the chorizo. Add 400 g can tomatoes and gradually add 4–5 cups stock, broccoli and 1–2 tablespoons chopped oregano, boiling gently and stirring occasionally. Cook until almost all the liquid has been absorbed.

- **GADO GADO.** Throw peanut sauce (¼ cup peanut paste, 2 tablespoons hoisin sauce, 1 tablespoon soy sauce and 1 crushed clove garlic with a little water and chilli and sugar to taste) over roughly chopped steamed vegies: 1 head broccoli, 2 carrots, 2 potatoes, 1 cup cabbage and 1 cup green beans. Add 2 quartered hard-boiled eggs. **If you have it:** Serve sprinkled with crushed peanuts.

- **ROAST.** Don't just steam broccoli, roast it in a little oil with:

  Lemon juice, lemon rind, chilli and almonds.

  Onion, bacon and pine nuts.

  Ginger. And just before serving dress with a mixture of soy sauce, sugar and a few drops of sesame oil.

  Cashews and garlic. And just before serving dress with a combination of soy sauce, vinegar and sugar.

- **ROASTED GARLIC SOUP.** Combine 1 large head coarsely chopped broccoli, 1 finely diced potato and 5 cups stock. Bring to a boil. Reduce heat, cover, and simmer until potato is tender, about 30 minutes. During the last 5 minutes, squeeze a whole bulb of roasted garlic into the pot. Puree.

- **SOUR CREAM AND CHEESE PASTA.** Broccoli makes a great pasta sauce. Add steamed broccoli to 1 cup sour cream, ¼ cup milk, 1 crushed clove garlic and 1 cup cheese, any variety – blue vein varieties are fabulous. **If you have it:** Add diced red capsicum, roasted is especially delicious.

Cake

From crummy to scrummy

Stale cake, sunken sponges and other baking disasters: let us show you how to turn them into sweet success. Your guests will be none the wiser.

Buried treasure

This story must take the cake when it comes to tales of longevity. In 1912 Sir Douglas Mawson buried leftover plum puddings in the Antarctic snow. In 1950 he received word that French expeditioners had come across the 38-year-old 'delicacies' and eaten them. With gusto.

Storing

For cakes and muffins, the general rule is to store in an airtight container at room temperature. The fridge tends to dry them out. However, if they contain anything perishable, like cream cheese, then in the fridge they should go.

If you've baked your own cake, don't cover until it's completely cooled or it will sweat. Add any filling at the last minute.

Freezing: Wrap really well to avoid freezer burn – in plastic wrap and then in foil.

Variety	Room temperature	Fridge	Freezer
Fruit cake (not iced)	1 month		up to 1 year
Most cakes	5–7 days		up to 3 months
Cheesecake		3–4 days	2–3 months
Muffins	3 days		2 months
Scones	1–2 days		2 months

A PIECE OF (WEDDING) CAKE

To save the top layer of a wedding cake for a 1st anniversary celebration, make sure it's sitting on plastic or foil (not cardboard). Freeze the cake uncovered for an hour to harden the icing. Then wrap in plastic wrap, making sure it's airtight, and double wrap in foil. Put in a container and freeze.

Using Up

- **APPLE TRIFLE.** Put cubes of leftover sponge or fruit cake in the bottom of a dish and top with apple sauce (see p. 7). Pour over custard, sprinkle with toasted almonds and chill.
- **CAKE BASE.** Mix melted butter into crumbled leftover cake for a base for frozen desserts or unbaked cheesecakes.
- **FRUIT CAKE FUDGE.** Heat 1½ tablespoons butter, 1½ tablespoons golden syrup and 2 tablespoons brown sugar until melted. Add 2 cups crumbled fruit cake and ¼ cup cocoa or drinking chocolate. Mix well and cook for a minute or two. Spread mixture on a lightly greased baking sheet and chill for at least ½ hour in the fridge. Cut into squares.
- **HOT CAKE.** Pour some orange juice over stale slices of sponge or fruit cake. Heat in a moderate oven for 10 minutes and serve with custard and/or cream.
- **HOT TRIFLE.** Lay slices of cake in a dish and cover with custard or chocolate sauce and heat through.
- **LAMINGTONS.** Make up a packet jelly. Just as it's starting to set, dip in squares of leftover sponge cake and coat in coconut.
- **RUM BALLS.** Beat together ½ cup cream cheese and ¼ cup sifted icing sugar. Add 2 tablespoons melted dark chocolate, ¼ teaspoon vanilla and ½ teaspoon rum and mix thoroughly. Add 2 cups crumbled chocolate cake, ¾ cup desiccated coconut and ¼ cup sultanas that have been soaked in 1½ tablespoons dark rum. Chill mixture in fridge. Form into balls and roll in chocolate sprinkles or coconut.
- **STEAMED DELIGHT.** Cut dry fruit cake into decent-sized slices, wrap in foil and steam over a pot of water.
- **SUGARY SLICES.** Fry thinnish slices of Christmas pudding in hot butter for a minute on each side. Sprinkle with caster sugar and serve hot or cold.
- **TRIFLE.** The basic dish is a layer of leftover sponge cake, a layer of fruit, a thin layer of jelly, a layer of custard and a layer of cream. Pour the jelly in gradually, letting it soak into the

cake until there's a centimetre or so above the fruit. Let it set before adding custard. Try leftover chocolate cake with jam instead of fruit.

- **TRUFFLES.** Gradually moisten 2 cups chocolate-cake crumbs with strong cold coffee (about ¼ cup) and grated rind 1 orange until you can form a ball. Roll into small balls and chill them in the fridge, then roll in cocoa powder or melted chocolate. **If you have it:** Add slivered almonds, or replace orange rind with peppermint essence. Press the mixture around raisins or glacé cherries. Roll in chocolate sprinkles.

A Little Effort

- **BAKED ALASKA.** A sunken sponge cake is ideal for this recipe. Put canned or fresh fruit in the sunken bit and top with ice-cream. Cover the lot with stiff meringue (see p. 109). Bake in hot oven for 1–2 minutes and serve immediately.

- **FRUIT CAKE STRUDEL.** Prepare filo pastry as instructed on the packet, using 4 sheets. Combine 3 cups crumbled fruit cake or Christmas pudding with 250 grams ricotta cheese and the zest 1 orange. Put mixture on pastry, folding sides over mixture and roll up. Transfer strudel, seam side down, to buttered baking dish and brush with an egg beaten with 1 teaspoon water. Sprinkle with a little cinnamon and brown sugar. Cut some steam vents. Bake in moderately hot oven until golden (15 minutes). Dust with sugar and serve with cream and/or ice-cream.

- **MEGA JAM TART.** The cake is ruined. It didn't bake well or it just wasn't nice. Our solution? Rip it up into coarse cake crumbs and turn it into dessert. Pre-prepare a homemade base or follow instructions on packet. Spread jam over pastry base. Fold the cake crumbs and 1 cup desiccated coconut into a stiffly beaten eggwhite. Pour mixture over jam. Bake in a moderate oven until the topping is cooked (about 20 minutes). Dust with icing sugar.

- **PANETTONE PUDDING.** Old panettone makes a mean bread pudding (see p. 35). **If you have it:** Try toasted slices of stale chocolate cake for a really decadent version. (See p. 202 for something a bit different.)

A LOAD OF WAFFLE

Apparently waffles were invented quite by accident when a weary Scotsman in medieval times sat down. He left the impression of his armour on his wife's recently baked cakes.

Biscuits

Storing

General advice is to store biscuits in airtight containers. Some swear by lining container with paper towel, greaseproof paper or even foil. You could try a couple of sugar cubes in the container to absorb moisture.

Don't store soft and crisp biscuits together; the crisp ones will go soggy.

For home-baked biscuits, make sure they're completely cooled before covering or they'll sweat.

WASTE WARRIOR TIP

If you live in a humid place, save those little packets of silica gel that you get in some pre-packaged foods and pop one in the biscuit barrel. It will stop your biscuits going moist and sticky.

Rescue remedies

- If your soft biscuits have begun to dry out, put a piece of apple or a slice of bread in the container for 24 hours.
- If your crisp biscuits have become soggy, put them in a low oven for a few minutes just before serving. You can only do this once.

Freezing: In airtight containers or plastic bags for up to 12 months. Put waxed paper between the layers.

Using Up

- **BROKEN BISCUIT SLICE.** Gently melt 100 grams butter, 2 tablespoons caster sugar and 1 tablespoon golden syrup. Don't let it boil. Stir in 2 cups broken biscuits, 2 tablespoons cocoa and ⅓ cup sultanas. Line 20 cm square dish with plastic wrap or greaseproof paper. Press cake mixture into dish. Melt 100 grams chocolate and spread over mixture. Chill until firm and cut into squares. **If you have it:** Add chopped dried apricots and/or pecan nuts to the mixture.
- **ICE-CREAM.** Make cassata by adding crushed sweet biscuits and a teaspoon of vanilla essence to a ½ tub of vanilla ice-cream.

BISCUIT BASE

All those broken biscuits and crumbs at the bottom of the biscuit packet need not go to waste. Collect in the freezer until you have enough to make a base for a flan or cheesecake.

For a 250 gram packet of biscuits, you need about 125 grams butter. Crush the biscuits to fine breadcrumbs. Add the melted butter. Press into flan or cake tin and chill for at least an hour before filling.

Capsicum

Catch that leftover piece before it withers

This is where you find out how to pick and peel a peck of peppers. Don't get left with half a capsicum lurking at the back of the fridge, slowly shrivelling up around the edges.

DID YOU KNOW?

By 'peck' we mean 'a lot'. We don't imagine many of you will be grappling with the actual metric equivalent of a peck, which is 10 litres worth.

Buying

Most capsicums start life as green ones, changing as they ripen to red, yellow, orange or purple, depending on variety.

The freshest capsicums have green stems and feel heavy for their size.

Season: Available all year. Best value from November to June.

Colour	Uses
Green	Fresh 'raw' flavour is ideal for quick-cook recipes like stir-fry
Yellow and orange	Sweet and colourful in salads
Red	The sweetest Most popular for stuffed and roast capsicum

Storing

Whole: In a plastic bag in the vegetable crisper. Green capsicum stays fresh for about a week, a little longer than the others. Make sure it is dry.

Cut: Wrap the cut end in a paper towel to absorb moisture. Store in main section of the fridge because the crisper can be a bit damp.

Roasted: In sealed container in the fridge. But the best place is the freezer where capsicums keep for up to nine months in a plastic container. Try storing between layers of waxed paper to easily pull apart.

Pickled peppers

Let's hope the peppers Peter Piper picked were pickled properly. If not, they can cause botulism. If you intend to preserve capsicum in oil or vinegar or a mixture of the two, follow recipe directions well. And store your jars in the fridge. Refer to CSIRO guidelines at www.csiro.au/resources/preservation-in-oil-vinegar.html

Freezing: Very easy and works well. There's no need to blanch. Just chop and freeze. It won't be crisp when it thaws, but it will still have the flavour. You can pop it still frozen into stews and soups and onto pizzas.

How much

1 cup chopped capsicum	= 125 grams
1 medium chunky capsicum	= 210 grams

Always slice on the inside to stop your knife slipping.

Using Up

Half a Cranky Capsicum

- **COLESLAW.** Combine sliced green capsicum with shredded cabbage, grated carrot and mayonnaise. **If you have it:** Add finely sliced onion.
- **DIP.** Cut into decent-sized strips to scoop up your favourite dips.
- **PIZZA.** Cut into strips and add to your favourite topping. Spread pizza base with 125 grams ricotta cheese and top with 1 cup roast pumpkin pieces, capsicum strips, 100 grams shaved ham and ¼ cup shaved parmesan. Bake for 10 minutes or so. Sprinkle with basil leaves before serving.
- **RATATOUILLE.** The ratatouille recipe (see p. 224) is just as nice with an extra portion of capsicum.
- **RICE-PAPER ROLLS.** Along with a couple of strips of capsicum, top rice paper with shredded lettuce, cooked chicken, a couple of carrot strips, a few bean sprouts and 2–3 coriander leaves. Fold sides in and roll up firmly.
- **RICE SALAD.** Combine 150 grams chopped cooked ham, sliced red capsicum, a handful of rocket leaves, 300 g can corn kernels and ¼ cup shaved parmesan. Mix through 3–4 cups cooked rice. Add a dressing of ½ cup olive oil and 2 tablespoons red wine vinegar and toss to combine. Serve warm or cold. Also check out other rice salads: a caramelised onion version (see p. 180) and a fruit and nut one (see p. 208).
- **ROAST.** Coat bite-sized pieces with oil and put in oven with other roast vegies for the last 20 minutes. **If you have it:** Combine with pitted and chopped black olives and/or a spoonful of capers.
- **SHASLIKS.** Thread capsicum cubes onto skewers with other vegies and/or meat, brush with olive oil and pop on the barbie or under the griller. Try combining with onion, mushroom and tomato pieces and chicken that's been marinated for an hour or so in a mixture of 3 tablespoons lemon juice, 1 tablespoon soy sauce and a splash of chilli sauce.

Colour power

Don't underestimate the power of adding a little colour. A few strips of less than perfect capsicum can enliven many dishes. Throw matchstick-sized slices into salads, vegetables, chicken or fish before serving. Or add near the end of cooking to beans, broccoli, cabbage or cauliflower.

- **STIR-FRY.** A colourful addition to any stir-fry recipe. Sauté 1 thickly sliced onion in a little oil, add 1 crushed clove garlic and 2 tablespoons sesame seeds until onion is golden. Add ½ chopped red capsicum, 1 carrot cut into julienne strips and 1 cup cauliflower florets and cook until tender. Add 1½ cups shredded cabbage along with ¼ cup hoisin sauce. Stir until cooked through.

A Peck of Peppers (otherwise known as a glut ...)

Okay, you've succumbed to the spiel and bought a big bag of capsicums at the market. Now what do you do? We say bake them, stew them, roast them and, well, stuff 'em.

- **CAPSICUM LAMB.** Sauté 1 small chopped onion and 2 cloves crushed garlic until soft. Add 500 grams lamb fillets cut into small cubes and cook until browned on all sides. Add 2 tablespoons fresh rosemary and ¾ cup red wine. Simmer for a few minutes. Add 3 sliced capsicums (try 1 red, 1 yellow and 1 green) and 3–4 chopped tomatoes. Simmer for 30 minutes.
- **CAPSICUM STEW.** Cut up and sauté 6 small potatoes in oil with 1 finely chopped red onion and 2 crushed cloves garlic until soft and golden (about 15 minutes). Add 400 g can tomatoes, 1 tablespoon tomato paste and 6 capsicums, cut into strips lengthwise (try 3 red and 3 yellow). Cook gently for about 15 minutes. Add ⅓ cup pitted black olives and ¾ cup fresh basil. Continue cooking until vegetables are soft but not mushy. Season and serve stew with a garnish of basil leaves.

Roasted Capsicum

How much

2 medium capsicums = 1 full cup roasted capsicum

Red is most commonly used, but there's nothing to stop you using others. Roast strips (skin side up) either under the griller or in a moderately hot oven. They're done when most of the skin bubbles and some are turning black.

To make them easy to peel, pop hot capsicum into a plastic bag for 10 minutes. Pull away skin and slice capsicums into thin strips.

- **CAPSICUM SAUCE.** For every cup of roasted red capsicum you need 1 tablespoon each olive oil and balsamic vinegar. Blend the lot until smooth. Spread on a pizza base, serve as a dip or use like tomato sauce. **If you have it:** Add some roasted garlic, a few chopped black olives or a dash of Tabasco.
- **DIP.** Blend 1½ cups roasted red capsicum, 125 grams cream cheese, 2 crushed cloves garlic and ½ cup basil until smooth. Stir through another ⅓ cup finely chopped basil. Refrigerate for 1 day to get the full flavour.
- **PESTO.** Blend 1 cup roasted red capsicum, 2 cloves garlic, 2 tablespoons parmesan and 2 tablespoons roasted pine nuts and slowly add olive oil until it forms a good paste. Serve with pasta. **If you have it:** Add cooked spinach to pasta.
- **SOUP.** Sauté 2 chopped red onions and 2–3 crushed cloves garlic in a little oil for a few minutes until light brown. Add 5 chopped tomatoes and cook for another 2 minutes. Add 1½ cups roasted red capsicum. Heat 2 cups chicken stock. Blend stock with sautéed mixture. Serve hot or cold.

Stuffed Capsicum

Cut off top, take out seeds and stuff cavity with your favourite filling. Replace lids, brush all over with olive oil and bake in a moderately hot oven for 45 minutes. If they won't sit straight trim a sliver from the base to stabilise them. Or prop them up with potato wedges.

- **MINI SHEPHERD'S PIE.** Fill ¾ of the capsicum with leftover spaghetti bolognaise mixture, top with mashed potato and sprinkle with grated cheese.
- **SAVOURY FILLING.** Sauté 2–3 rashers chopped bacon, 1 chopped onion and ½ cup mushrooms. Shouldn't need to add any oil. Stir through 1½ cups soft breadcrumbs, 1 chopped tomato and 1 tablespoon fresh herbs. Top with dried breadcrumbs.
- **TUNA MORNAY.** Fill capsicum with a mixture of leftover tuna mornay and cooked rice. Top with grated cheese.
- **TOMATO.** Lots of spare tomatoes too? Make a sauce and pour over stuffed capsicums. Pop some halved tomatoes between them to roast.
- **MORE IDEAS.** Find more suggestions with rice (see p. 208) and bread (see p. 38).

Carrot

Ideas from around the world

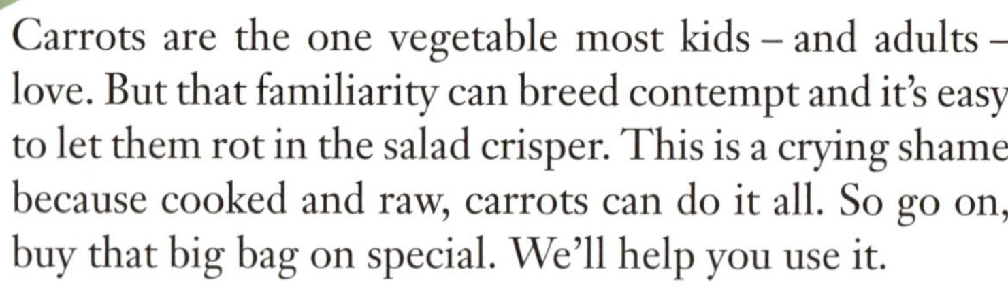

Carrots are the one vegetable most kids – and adults – love. But that familiarity can breed contempt and it's easy to let them rot in the salad crisper. This is a crying shame because cooked and raw, carrots can do it all. So go on, buy that big bag on special. We'll help you use it.

Buying

Carrots with lots of little roots or large green areas at the top are probably getting old.

Go for most colourful if considering nutrition.

Any tops should be bright green and feathery.

Season: Carrots are grown all year round but still cheaper in their traditional season of March to August.

RAW SURPRISE

Unlike most other vegetables, carrots are actually more nutritious cooked than raw.

This is because cooking – and juicing – breaks down the carrot's tough cellular walls and releases more betacarotene (which is converted to Vitamin A in your body). Try not to peel your carrots as most of this nutrition is in the skin, or just below it.

Storing

Whole: Carrots are the prima donnas of the vegetable kingdom; they rot if they get too wet and wilt if they get too dry. Keep them in fridge – the vegetable crisper is perfect – in a plastic bag with a few holes in it, or wrap in a paper towel and then put in the bag. Carrots keep at least a week, up to three.

If you bought carrots with tops, cut them off – they'll age the carrots faster.

> **The carrot is there to provide energy for the leaf. When it's in the ground, the whole idea is to make the top look nice. That's the point for the carrot. But for us, the carrot is to eat.** **Greengrocer**

DID YOU KNOW?

Carrots are thought to have been originally red, black or purple and probably came from Afghanistan. It was the Dutch who developed the orange variety in the 16th and 17th centuries. The different colours are still around, including purple, but only available in specialty shops.

They can become bitter if they come into contact with fruit that produces the ripening gas, ethylene. You risk this happening if you throw carrots loose into the crisper with apples and pears, for example. But it's easily solved if you keep them in separate plastic bags.

Cut: If your carrots are a bit floppy and you're not ready to eat them yet, try cutting into sticks and putting them in a bowl of water. You'll get a few more days out of them, at the very least.

Freezing: Good, but you have to cook them a little first. Boil or steam for a few minutes and throw in airtight containers in the portion sizes you'll later need. Then you can toss straight from the freezer into the cooking pot. Carrots frozen this way take about half the cooking time compared with fresh.

Meals containing carrots freeze well.

WASTE WARRIOR TIP

Yes, you can eat the tops but they may be an acquired taste as they are rather bitter. (Carrots are in the same family as parsley and celery.) Carrot tops wilt quickly, so if you're planning to throw them in a salad it should be on the same day you cut them.

How much

1 medium carrot = 125 grams
= 1 cup grated carrot

The clever con and carrots

If you think carrots can help you see in the dark – you've been had! But don't worry, you're not alone. The myth that carrots give you night vision was invented during World War II by the British air force. They were using radar, a new technology, to shoot down German planes but they wanted to hide this from the enemy. No one told the locals it was a ruse so British civilians went crazy planting carrots so they could see during blackouts.

Using Up

One Cranky Carrot

- **FRITTATA/COOKED SLICE.** Add grated carrot to spinach or zucchini slice for a balancing sweetness (see p. 225).
- **MASHED POTATO.** Replace some of the potatoes with carrots for a sweet change. Add a dash of coconut milk and sprinkle of coriander for an unforgettable mash.
- **MEAT LOAF/HAMBURGERS/RISSOLES/MEATBALLS/ BOLOGNAISE SAUCE.** Replace up to half the meat with grated carrot – it's slightly sweeter and much healthier.
- **NEAPOLITANA PASTA SAUCE.** Grate into tomato-based sauces. The carrot helps the sauce stick to the pasta.
- **SOUPS.** Chop and pop into pretty much any soup. Think pumpkin, tomato, capsicum, fennel, cauliflower, chicken noodle, lamb hotpot and seafood chowder. Chop finely and add to sautéing onions and garlic as a basis for soups, casseroles and stews.
- **STIR-FRY.** Julienne into small strips and throw into any stir-fry from beef to tofu.
- **TOAST/SANDWICHES.** Process cooked carrot in food processor with a couple of mint leaves, a few drops of olive oil and few drops of lemon juice. Spread on sourdough toast. Grate raw carrot and add to peanut paste sandwiches.

HANDY HINT

Carrots make sensational chips. Treat just like potatoes. They also crisp up really well if they are already cooked, so chips are a great solution for leftovers.

Also, roast or fry carrot peels for a delicious garnish you can eat.

If you're putting a carrot in a stew put it in whole. Don't peel it, don't cut it. When it's soft, fish it out and mash it up, it gives a nice texture. **Marjorie**

A Couple of Cranky Carrots

- **CARROT CAKE.** Beat together 1¼ cups sugar and ¾ cup oil. Add 3 eggs gradually and mix well. Add 1½ cups flour, 1½ teaspoons baking powder, 1 teaspoon bicarbonate of soda, 1 teaspoon cinnamon and 1 tablespoon finely chopped glacéd ginger (or 1 tablespoon powdered). Add 2½ cups grated carrot and 1 cup sultanas and stir until just combined. Bake for 55–60 minutes in a moderate oven. Great with cream cheese frosting. Combine 250 grams cream cheese (low-fat works just as well), 1 tablespoon lemon juice or 1 teaspoon vanilla and ½ cup icing sugar.

- **CARROT AND LENTIL PATTIES.** Mash 2 grated carrots with 400 g can brown lentils, 3 finely chopped spring onions, 1 tablespoon tomato paste, 1 teaspoon grated lemon zest, 1 lightly beaten egg and ¼ cup breadcrumbs. Shape the mixture into 8 patties. Coat each in a further ¼ cup breadcrumbs. Fry 2 minutes each side or until browned, or spray with cooking oil and bake in moderate oven. Serve with yoghurt flavoured with crushed garlic. **If you have it:** Add ¼ cup chopped parsley, basil or coriander. Or use other grated vegies like zucchini or sweet potato.

- **COOKED SALAD.** Yes, you can make salad out of slightly old carrots. Just steam and slice. For 3 carrots, add ¼ cup sultanas and dress with 1 tablespoon lemon juice, 3 tablespoons olive oil, ¼ teaspoon paprika, ¼ teaspoon cumin and ¼ cup coriander.

- **HUMMUS.** Blend 2 cooked carrots with 400 g can chickpeas, 2 tablespoons tahini, 1 clove garlic, 1 tablespoon each lemon juice and water. Spread on sandwiches, pita bread, salmon steaks and lamb cutlets.

- **LEMONADE CARROTS.** Decadent but divine. Works with flat lemonade or champagne. For 3 carrots: make a white sauce with 1½ tablespoons flour and 50 grams butter. Cook and stir for 2 minutes before adding 1 cup chicken stock and ½ cup lemonade. Bring to boil, stirring, until thickened. Add sliced carrots. Cook until carrots are soft. (For sweet tooths, vary the proportions of lemonade to stock.)

- **PICKLED CARROT.** Great with cold meats or in sandwiches. Heat 2 thinly sliced carrots with 1 cup vinegar, 2 tablespoons sugar and 1 teaspoon mustard seeds and stir until sugar dissolves. Leave for 1–2 hours before serving. Makes about 1½ cups. **If you have it:** Replace some of the carrots with green beans or zucchini.

A Lot of Cranky Carrots

- **SOUP.** So easy, so good. Sauté 1 sliced onion and 1 crushed clove garlic in a little oil with a couple of teaspoons of curry spices; any combination of ginger, cumin, coriander and/or curry powder. Add 5 cups stock, 5 carrots and 1 potato. Cook until vegetables are soft. Blend. **If you have it:** Add coconut milk and chopped coriander.

- **CARROT AND COTTAGE CHEESE TRIANGLES.** An easy filling for filo pastry. Prepare filo as instructed on the packet, cutting sheets into 4. For 4 grated carrots add 180 g tub cottage cheese, 1 lightly beaten egg, 2–3 tablespoons each chopped spring onions, pine nuts and parmesan. Put spoonfuls of mixture on pastry, fold over and seal. Bake in moderate oven 20 minutes or until browned.

- **CARROT HALWA.** Very sweet, very more-ish Indian/Pakistani sweet. Keeps in fridge for up to a week. Cook 4 grated carrots in 1 tablespoon butter for a few minutes. Add 400 g can condensed milk, 1 cup water and ½–1 teaspoon cinnamon or cardamom, depending on your preference. Stir occasionally until nearly all liquid has evaporated. Stir in 1–2 cups slivered almonds and/or pistachios. (Raisins and sultanas work well too.) Serve hot or roll into balls and drop into patty pans and decorate each with a spare nut.

- **MARMALADE.** Not just for toast but also to glaze roast chicken and to top cakes and steamed puddings. Bring to boil 4–5 carrots, the zest and juice 1 orange, 1½ cups sugar, 1 cup water and ½ teaspoon cinnamon. Simmer, partially covered, for 1 hour until it's the consistency of thin honey. Makes about 2 cups.

Cauliflower

No need to hide this beauty under a sauce

Polishing off a whole cauliflower in one sitting takes a lot of dedication or a lot of diners. It's easy to get caught with a half going floppy in the crisper. To use it up, don't just think cheese. Cauliflower is one of the great chameleons in the kitchen.

Buying

If the leaves are fresh, that's a great indication that the florets are as well. So look for green, firm leaves.

As well as the white cauliflower, you may come across green and purple. **Broccoflower** are bright green. They're a cross with broccoli but they taste primarily like cauliflower.

Jacaranda purple cauliflowers contain a red pigment found in other red-coloured fruits and vegetables. The purple colour fades on cooking but they're a little sweeter than the white or green caulies.

Season: Available all year around but best value between May and November.

WASTE WARRIOR TIP

You can eat the leaves *and* the stem of the cauliflower. Chop and cook just like the florets. If you're growing your own, you can also eat all those big dark green leaves around the vegetable that never make it to the supermarket. But be quick, they get a bit tough and bitter as they get older.

Storing

Whole: In plastic bags in the fridge with the stem side down to prevent moisture developing in the florets. But try not to store cauliflower in the coldest part of the fridge. It's susceptible to chilling damage and then it can rot. It keeps for one or two weeks.

Cut: Florets don't last as long after you've cut them up, just a few days in an airtight container in the fridge.

Cooked: Lasts two to three days in an airtight container in the fridge.

Freezing: Pretty good. Blanch for three minutes in boiling water or steam for five minutes and then freeze. Once thawed, the cauliflower is a bit watery, but fine in combination dishes.

Using

How much

1 cauliflower (florets only)	= 750 grams
1 cauliflower (including stem)	= 1 kilogram
1 medium cauliflower	= 4 cups florets

The key to cooking cauliflower is not to overdo it. The longer you cook it, the more it smells – and tastes – like boiled cabbage (it is in the same family, after all).

Also, the older the cauliflower, the more likely it is to taste stronger.

In most recipes broccoli and cauliflower may be substituted for one another, so check broccoli chapter too.

DID YOU KNOW?

Cauliflower isn't really a flower at all but a bunch of stems. The real flowers grow out of the white heads on thin stalks (at which point the vegetable is too old to be good to eat). Broccoli is different though, the florets are the flowers.

All white on its own

You don't have to do anything to keep your cauliflower white during cooking.

Despite persistent rumours that you do, you don't need lemon juice, milk, flour or vinegar for creamy florets. But do be careful with aluminium pans. They can turn cauliflower grey.

Using Up

A Few Floppy Florets

- **CURRY.** Throw florets into virtually any Indian-style curry as they absorb the flavours beautifully. Teams well with coriander and mint. Good addition to lentil-based dhal.
- **CRUSTLESS VEGETABLE QUICHE.** Add 2 cups cold steamed vegetables (like cauliflower, pumpkin and zucchini) to 4 lightly beaten eggs, 1½ cups milk and ½ cup self-raising flour and 1½ cups grated cheese. Bake in a moderate oven for 40 minutes or until just set.
- **MASH/SHEPHERD'S PIE.** Add to mashed potato. Top off shepherd's pie with cauliflower instead of potatoes – or a combination of the two.
- **MIXED GREEN SALAD.** Lightly steamed florets can be added to salad greens. They'll absorb any salad dressing and blend in well. Cauli also goes well with tomatoes.
- **PASTA.** Add to baked pasta dishes, like macaroni cheese and bacon.
- **STEWS, CASSEROLES, SOUPS.** Cauliflower disappears but bulks out and lightens up many slow-cooked dishes.
- **STIR-FRY.** Chop and toss through combination stir-fry, keeping it crunchy.

Half a Large Floppy Head

- **ANCHOVY PASTA.** This is even better with an old cauliflower that might have a really strong flavour because it can compete with the anchovies. Sauté 1 chopped onion in a little oil, add 1 crushed clove garlic, 4–6 mashed anchovies and chilli to taste. Be generous with the cooking oil. Add cauliflower florets, ½ cup white wine and ½ cup stock, cover and lightly steam. Toss with cooked pasta. **If you have it:** Add chopped parsley.

- **ASIAN SIDE DISH.** Sauté in a little oil with ginger and onion. Add a couple of tablespoons of stock and 1 tablespoon each oyster and soy sauce. Cover and steam until just soft.
- **COCONUT AND APPLE CURRY.** Sauté 1 onion and 2 crushed cloves garlic in a little oil. Add 1 tablespoon curry paste and cook for 1 minute. Add the cauliflower florets, 1 head chopped broccoli, 1 diced apple and 1 cup each stock and coconut milk. Cover and cook until tender. Serve with chopped coriander and roasted cashews.
- **FRIED.** Dip slightly steamed florets into egg and then breadcrumbs spiced with garlic, ginger and chilli. Pan-fry, turning to brown all sides. **If you have it:** Add some spring onions and soy sauce to frypan for a minute at the end of cooking. Serve with minty yoghurt.
- **FRIED 'RICE'.** An unusual solution for leftover cooked cauliflower is to treat it like cold cooked rice. For every cup of cauliflower, add 1 egg, fried and sliced into strips, ¼ cup cooked peas, 20 grams finely chopped ham, ½ onion sautéed in a little oil and ¼ grated carrot. Heat in frypan and add a generous splash of soy and/or hoisin sauce.
- **HORSERADISH PUREE/SOUP.** A vegetable side dish or a soup. Puree steamed cauliflower, butter-sautéed onions and a splash of cream or milk. Add 1–2 teaspoons horseradish cream. Serve like mashed potato. For soup, add stock. Use cooked potato if you don't have enough cauliflower. **If you have it:** Replace horseradish with mustard or toasted caraway or fennel seeds. **Second helpings:** Toss through just-cooked pasta and serve with grated cheese and chopped chives.
- **ITALIAN-STYLE TOMATO.** Sauté 1 chopped onion and 1 crushed clove garlic in a little oil. Add cauliflower florets and 400 g can tomatoes, ¼ cup water, 1 tablespoon Worcestershire sauce, a handful black olives and 1 tablespoon chopped oregano. Simmer, covered, for 10 minutes until tender. Terrific side dish for beef and lamb.
- **MUSTARD PICKLES.** Sauté a couple of chopped onions in a little oil and add cauliflower/carrots/beans, ½ cup sugar, 1 teaspoon each black peppercorns and mustard seeds and 1 tablespoon dry mustard. Add 1¾ cups white wine vinegar and

simmer about 10 minutes. Add 1 tablespoon plain flour which has been blended with ¼ cup white wine vinegar. Stir until it thickens. Keeps in the fridge for at least a week.

- **PEA FRITTERS.** Great dish when you don't seem to have anything in the fridge. You'll need frozen peas and an egg. Steam cauliflower and ½ cup frozen peas and mash. Add to ½ cup flour with 1½ teaspoons cumin, ½ teaspoon cinnamon and ½ teaspoon turmeric. Stir in lightly beaten egg. Roll a heaped tablespoon into a ball, flatten and fry until golden on both sides. Serve with yoghurt and chopped coriander.

- **ROASTED.** One of the tastiest ways to eat cauliflower – and easiest. Chop, drizzle with oil and bake in a hot oven until lightly golden and just tender. Try:

  Olives and garlic. Roast with ½ cup quartered olives and 1–2 crushed cloves garlic. Once cooked toss with a couple of tablespoons of toasted breadcrumbs and chopped parsley. **If you have it:** Add 1 tablespoon chopped rinsed capers.

  Roasted chickpea salad. Roasted cauliflower combines beautifully with chickpeas. Combine with 400 g can chickpeas, 1 chopped tomato, the zest and juice 1 lemon, a handful of chopped parsley, another tablespoon or two of oil and ½ teaspoon cumin.

  Roasted tomato curry. Roast 2–3 chopped carrots along with cauliflower. Sauté 2 chopped onions in a little oil with 3 crushed cloves garlic. Add ¼ teaspoon each turmeric, cumin and garam masala, ½ teaspoon coriander and chilli to taste. Fry until fragrant. Add carrots, cauliflower and half a 400 g can tomatoes. Cook for a few minutes. Serve with chopped coriander.

Celery

Who uses even half a bunch in one go?
What to do with the rest

DID YOU KNOW?

It may look like it, but celeriac is not the celery root. However it is a type of celery. It's the swollen bottom of the stem, or the corm. It's the result of selective breeding, growers deliberately choosing the plants that developed the corm. It has a milder flavour than celery stalks and makes a great mash.

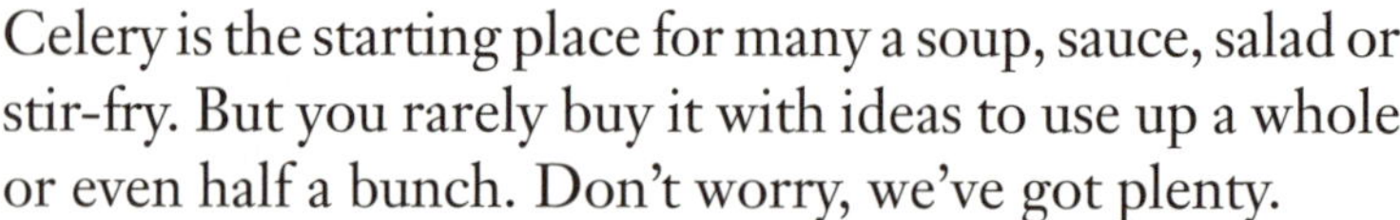

Celery is the starting place for many a soup, sauce, salad or stir-fry. But you rarely buy it with ideas to use up a whole or even half a bunch. Don't worry, we've got plenty.

> **Celery is the one green salad ingredient I can put in a salad today and will be just as good tomorrow. It won't go soggy like lettuce will.**
> **Terese**

Buying

Avoid stalks that freely move away from the bunch. Celery should smell fresh, not musty.

Season: Available all year round.

Skinny myth

The idea that celery contains 'negative kilojoules' is a myth. You don't get skinnier the more you eat. It does seem like hard work chewing through celery sometimes, but you don't burn up more energy eating and digesting celery than the vegetable contains.

Storing

WASTE WARRIOR TIP

Slice stalks of celery and store in the juice of your store-bought pickles or gherkins. The celery takes on the flavour of the pickling juice but retains some crunch, even after days of soaking.

Whole: In the crisper, either in a plastic bag with a few holes or just pull a plastic bag over each end. There's a splinter group of you that swear by foil but our (admittedly quite unscientific) experiments show it doesn't work as well. Keep celery away from the coldest part of your fridge as celery can freeze and be damaged. It keeps for up to two weeks.

If the stalks start to wilt, pull them off and stick them in a bowl of ice-water for at least an hour. Or, use cold water and put the bowl in the fridge.

Cut: In an airtight container in the fridge. You can keep celery slices in cold water too, but you'll need to keep changing the water.

Freezing: Don't bother. The result is a useless mash. However, you can get away with it if it's finely chopped up in a dish.

Using

How much

2 large stalks of celery = 1 cup

Using Up

- **AU GRATIN.** Sauté 6 thickly sliced stalks with 1 chopped onion in 1–2 tablespoons butter. Cover with ½ cup stock and ¼ cup white wine. Combine ⅓ cup walnuts, 1 cup breadcrumbs and 1 tablespoon butter. Sprinkle over celery. Bake in moderately hot oven until the celery is soft. **If you have it:** Add a dash of cream to the cooking broth.
- **BOLOGNAISE.** Grate into bolognaise sauce.
- **BRAISED CELERY.** Remove as many strings as you can (try a vegetable peeler) from 8 stalks, chop into large pieces and cover with beef stock, about ½–⅔ cup. Cover dish and bake in hot oven until just tender. Remove cover and let stock reduce to glaze. **If you have it:** Add finely sliced onions or pancetta/bacon/ham or 1 crushed clove garlic. Replace some of the stock with white wine.
- **CAJUN FISH SIMMERING SAUCE.** Sauté 1 chopped onion, 1 chopped stick celery and 1 chopped capsicum in a little oil until softened. Add a couple of cups of chicken stock, 400 g can each tomatoes and sweetcorn, 1 tablespoon sugar and chilli to taste. Cook for a few minutes. Add 1 kilogram prawns or 4 white fish fillets and heat until they are cooked through. **If you have it:** Cook with thyme, bay leaf, and oregano. Add chopped basil and parsley.

- **CHILLI CREAM DIP.** Add a couple of thinly sliced stalks to ½ finely chopped red onion, a dash of sweet chilli sauce and a 250 g tub cream cheese.
- **CURRIED SOUP.** Sauté 1 onion and 1 crushed clove garlic in a little oil. Add 1 tablespoon curry powder and 2 teaspoons cumin. Cook until fragrant. Add 6 chopped stalks celery, 2 carrots, 1 cored and diced apple and 4 cups chicken stock. Cook until tender. Puree.
- **EGGPLANT SALAD.** Sauté 1 eggplant chopped into cubes until golden, add 2 crushed cloves garlic and 2 sticks finely chopped celery. Cook for about 10 minutes, until the eggplant is tender. Remove from heat. Stir in a couple of chopped tomatoes, 1 tablespoon balsamic vinegar, ¼ cup pine nuts, a dozen olives and ½ cup chopped chives. Serve chilled.
- **PICKLED CELERY.** Cook to soften slightly and toss with dressing of 1 tablespoon soy sauce, 1 tablespoon vinegar, ½ teaspoon salt, ½ teaspoon sugar and ½ teaspoon sesame oil. Refrigerate, covered for 30 minutes and serve.
- **PRAWN COCKTAIL.** Add finely chopped celery to a good egg mayonnaise with a splash of tomato puree and a dash of Tabasco. Pour over prawns.
- **RATATOUILLE.** Add a few stalks of chopped celery with the onions and garlic (see p. 224).
- **ROASTED.** Roast turkey or chicken on a bed of 4 stalks celery, 4–5 carrots and 3 quartered onions. The vegetables become roasted in chicken fat. Or throw celery, carrots and onions in for the last hour of roasting lamb.
- **SIDE DISH.** Sauté 1 chopped onion and 2–3 stalks finely chopped celery in a little oil until soft. Add a couple of cups of pearl barley, rice or lentils, then a few cups of stock and maybe ½ cup wine. Stir occasionally until cooked and liquid is absorbed. **If you have it:** Add chopped oregano.
- **SIMPLE COLESLAW.** Add thinly sliced celery to grated carrots. Make a dressing from natural yoghurt and a little mayonnaise. **If you have it:** Add chopped spring onions and strips of cooked chicken or turkey.

- **STIR-FRY BEEF.** Sauté 4 finely chopped celery stalks with 1 chopped onion and 1 crushed clove garlic, adding a few drops of sesame oil to the cooking oil. Add 500 grams thinly sliced beef and cook until browned. Add 3 tablespoons soy sauce, 1 tablespoon oyster sauce and 1 tablespoon stock. Stir-fry until the meat is cooked. Serve on steamed rice and sprinkle with almonds or sesame seeds.
- **STUFFED.** Fill the middle of trimmed stalks with cream cheese plus olives and walnuts. Or try any of these combinations: hummus and harissa paste; egg, mayonnaise and gherkins; or cream cheese, avocado and lemon juice.
- **STUFFING.** Sauté celery with the onion (see p. 37).

Sweet celery

In ancient Pompeii, celery was eaten as both a savoury and sweet dish. One dessert involved roasting celery and then seasoning it with honey and black pepper. Celery has long been candied, mainly for decoration. Today you can still buy candied Angelica (sometimes called wild celery) in some gourmet food stores. It comes from the same family as celery (and parsley) but tastes more like liquorice.

Cheese

Storing it so it lasts, using the pieces that don't
and how scared you should be
of the mouldy bits

So your cheese is so hard you could bounce it or so furry you could pet it. Is there a way to use it that tastes good and doesn't kill you? Yes, sometimes. But there's always a way to enjoy that slightly unusual cheese you bought as a one off and now have little idea what to do with.

WASTE WARRIOR TIP

Don't throw away that rind, no matter how hard it is.

- Pop straight into soup where it can slowly melt and add its flavour.
- Cover in olive oil. Add thyme or rosemary leaves and heat gently for 5–10 minutes. Cool. Grate over pizza, pasta or salads.

The stronger and tastier the cheese, the less you need to use. So I always buy the expensive stuff and use small amounts. Saves my waistline too. **Marianne**

Storing

Variety	Shelf life in fridge (after opening)
Creamy cheeses (ricotta, cottage)	Within a week
Cream cheese	up to 3 weeks
White mould (brie, camembert) Stretched curd (mozzarella, haloumi) Blue cheese	1–4 weeks
Cheddars and holey cheeses (gouda, edam)	Several weeks
Hard cheese (parmesan, romano)	Several months

Using Up

Top Tips for Any Old Cheese

Hot cheese

Some cheeses respond to cooking better than others. The best cooking cheeses are the harder ones, like parmesan, cheddar and Gruyere.

The flavour of cheese mellows on cooking, so you might want to choose a matured cheese with a stronger flavour.

- **CHEESE BALL.** Grate or mash any kind of cheese – about 125 grams worth – add ¼–½ cup chopped herbs and 1 tablespoon port, sherry or any other sweet fortified wine (or more if needed) to moisten. Shape into a ball, wrap in plastic and stick in the fridge for 1 hour. Remove and roll in nuts or cornflakes. Serve with crackers.
- **QUICHE.** All cheeses make great quiche. Pre-prepare a homemade base or follow instructions on packet. Fill with up to 125 grams cheese, any combination, mixed with 3 lightly whisked eggs, ½ cup milk and 1 bunch spring onions (sliced, green tops only). Bake in a moderately hot oven for 40 to 45 minutes until golden. Don't stop there: try blue cheese and broccoli; fetta and sun-dried tomato; gouda and mushroom; or camembert and caramelised onion.
- **SPANAKOPITA (SPINACH PIE).** This is a tasty way to use up a decent haul of odds and ends. Roughly mash about 200 grams soft cheese (like fetta, ricotta or blue cheese) with ¼ cup hard grated cheese (parmesan is great but edam works well too). Add 2 lightly whisked eggs, a pinch of nutmeg, 1½ tablespoons oil and 1 cup roughly chopped spinach. Line baking dish with 4 or 5 layers of filo (follow instructions on packet), pour filling in, repeat with another 4 or 5 buttered filo layers. Cook up to 1 hour in moderate oven.
- **TARTLETS.** These are great for a small amount of cheese that's gone hard or unappetising but is still safe to eat. Lightly whisk 6 eggs with ¼ cup cream and ¼ cup self-raising flour. Pour into mini muffin pans and drop a couple of squares of cheese into each and bake for 10–15 minutes until golden. **If you have it:** Add 1–2 tablespoons chopped herbs, a pinch of cayenne pepper, a splash of Tabasco or 2 teaspoons mustard.
- **VEGIE BAKE.** Can take any amount of any kind of cheese. Sauté 1 chopped onion in a little oil. Make up 1 cup in total cheese, any combination, with sour cream, cream and/or milk. Add to onion. Layer thinly sliced vegies (e.g. potato, carrot, broccoli) in a casserole dish and sprinkle over some of the creamy onion mixture. Repeat twice, then finish with a vegetable layer. Dot the top with butter. Bake in a moderate oven for 1 hour or until the vegetables are soft. **If you have it:** Stir 1 tablespoon tahini or tomato paste into the onion mixture. Sauté a couple of rashers of bacon with the onion.

Creamy cheeses –
Cottage Cheese, Cream Cheese, Mascarpone, Ricotta

Storing

Keep in the original container or a reusable plastic container with a lid.

With **ricotta**, drain off the whey – the clear liquid that can settle out – as it may sour the cheese. If you pack it in an airtight bag or tub, it will last longer.

If your cheese doesn't have an expiry date stamp, then use within the week. The exception is **cream cheese**. That can last two to three weeks after opening.

> **When you're handling cheese, make sure your hands are clean, and your board and your knife. That way there's no cross contamination so nothing can attach itself and grow.** **Cheese expert**

Freezing: Don't freeze mascarpone. Cottage cheese and cream cheese are best when frozen in cooked foods such as pastries and quiches. You can freeze ricotta but, once thawed, it's best only for cooking.

When is it past it?

If you see any mould on a creamy cheese, it is definitely time to throw it out. Don't try to salvage any of it.

Using Up

Top Tips for Creamy Cheeses

Take any combination.

- **BAKED.** Blend 1 cup cheese, ¼ cup caster sugar, 1 egg, 1 teaspoon vanilla extract and 1 tablespoon sultanas. Pour into muffin or cup-cake containers and bake in a moderately slow oven for about 45 minutes or until brown and the middle is just set. **If you have it:** Serve with stewed fruit.
- **DIPS.** If you can mash it, you can make a dip with it. If you need to bulk it out a little more, add mayonnaise, yoghurt and/or sour cream. For 125 grams cheese, add one of these flavourings: ¼ cup corn relish; ⅓ cup olive tapenade; ½ cup tomato salsa; or ¼ cup chopped herbs. (See pumpkin dip p. 139.)
- **PANCAKES.** Add 125 grams cheese to 1 beaten egg, 1 grated apple and 1¼ cups milk, 1 cup self-raising flour and 1 tablespoon sugar. Fry in butter until golden and bubbling and flip and repeat. Dust with cinnamon. **If you have it:** Replace the apples with mashed banana or any other fruit.
- **PARFAIT.** The ultimate no-cook using-up dessert. Beat 125 grams cheese with 150 grams icing sugar and 1 teaspoon vanilla essence until smooth. Alternate layers of fresh fruit with cheese mix and crumbled sweet biscuits. **If you have it:** Add in lemon or orange zest or cocoa powder to the cheese. Replace the icing sugar with jam. Make extra layers from custard, jelly and bite-sized cubes of cake.
- **PASTA.** Don't just think parmesan. Creamy cheeses are a sauce in themselves. Melt cheese with a little milk or stock over low heat. Add chopped herbs and pour over pasta. **If you have it:** Add olives, roasted peppers, anchovies, capers and tomatoes, fresh or canned. Try ¼ cup mascarpone, ¼ cup ricotta, 2 grated zucchini, 1 clove garlic and ¼ cup basil.
- **RISOTTO.** Finish your risotto with creamy cheese for a rich velvety taste. Add up to ½ cup.

- **SEAFOOD DRESSING.** To 125 grams cheese, add 1 tablespoon chopped dill and 1½ tablespoons lemon juice for cooked prawns or smoked salmon.
- **SOUP.** Creamy cheeses turn mushroom soup into cream of mushroom, turn pumpkin into cream of pumpkin; chicken . . . you get the picture and the taste! Or dollop a teaspoon into each serving bowl and sprinkle with fresh herbs. And don't just stop at soup; add to casseroles, curries and sauces. Just stir through up to ½ cup at the end of cooking.
- **SWEET DIP.** For dipping fresh fruit, blend ¼ cup fruit juice and ¼ cup honey with 125 grams cheese.

Mascarpone – a few extra ideas

- **CREAM.** Mascarpone can go anywhere cream can. That means hot chocolate and porridge as well as desserts.
- **SEAFOOD.** For a traditional Italian spread, combine ½ cup mascarpone with 3 finely chopped anchovies, 1 crushed clove garlic, ½ teaspoon mustard and ¼ cup chives and/or parsley.

WASTE WARRIOR WINNERS

Some of our best cheeses have come from leftovers and lucky accidents. Mascarpone was first invented as a way of using up the cream left over from the making of parmesan. Ricotta evolved as a use for the whey. Cottage cheese was probably discovered when warm milk was accidentally allowed to sour. (In the same way, we probably first came across cream cheese when cream was left to sour.) Blue cheese was likely a happy accident with a mould spore when the cheese was stored in a cave.

Fresh/Semi-Fresh Cheeses –

Fetta, Haloumi, Bocconcini/ Mozzarella

Buying

While bocconcini and mozzarella are the same cheese, the mozzarella you buy in Australia tends to be more aged than bocconcini and therefore lasts longer.

Avoid cheese where the brine or water solution is cloudy.

Storing

If the cheese is sold in brine, keep it fully immersed and in the fridge. If the water becomes cloudy, clean the container and replace with fresh water.

If the cheese comes in a dry vacuum-sealed pack, just cover the opened end with plastic wrap or put in an airtight container and store in the fridge.

Freezing: Don't freeze **haloumi**. **Fetta** can be frozen but afterward is best in cooked foods such as pastries and quiches. You can freeze grated **mozzarella** and **bocconcini**. But once thawed, they're best only for cooking.

When is it past it?

If you see any mould, it is definitely time to throw it out. Don't try to cut it off and salvage the rest of the batch.

Using Up

Top Tips for Fresh/Semi-Fresh Cheeses

Take any combination.

- **FRIED.** Dip bite-sized pieces of cheese in lightly beaten egg and then seasoned breadcrumbs or crushed almonds. Then deep fry or spray with oil and bake. Serve with toothpicks to dip in salsa or hot chilli sauce.
- **KEBAB.** Alternate cubes of cheese with chunks of bread and vegetables on a soaked wooden skewer. Marinate for 30 minutes. Fry or barbecue over high heat for 5–10 minutes, until some of the vegetables have started to brown. Try cheese, ribbons of zucchini (thread thick peeled slices onto the skewer), slices of Spanish onion and chunks of stale bread marinated in olive oil, lemon and thyme.
- **MARINATED.** Combine all the ingredients in a jar. Marinate overnight. You don't need much more for a pasta, pizza or salad dressing. For every 100 grams of cheese, add 1 teaspoon oregano or rosemary, 1 small finely sliced clove garlic, ½ teaspoon lemon rind and ½ cup olive oil. Keeps for a few weeks in the fridge.

Fetta – the salad cheese

- **SALAD DRESSING.** If you don't have enough fetta for the salad itself, add it to the dressing. Whisk ⅓ cup crumbled fetta, ¼ cup plain yoghurt, 1 tablespoon lemon juice, 1 tablespoon oil and 1 crushed clove garlic. **If you have it:** Add chopped mint, dill or basil.

Haloumi – a few extra ideas

- **DESSERT.** Dress grilled haloumi with 2 tablespoons honey and 1 tablespoon each lemon juice, toasted nuts and chopped mint.
- **FRITTERS.** Grate 1 carrot, 1 zucchini and 100 grams haloumi into 1 lightly whisked egg. Fry heaped tablespoons each side until golden. Serve with fetta dressing as above.

White Mould Cheese –
Brie, Camembert, Triple Cream

Buying

You don't have to worry about whether your cheese is ripe with many of the mainstream supermarket choices nowadays. Check the packaging, if it says 'ready to eat' (or something similar) it's been aged to a certain point and held there for a time so it lasts longer. (It will, of course, eventually ripen and age.)

RIPE AND READY

If you've bought a more traditional cheese, it's ripe when it's soft from the edge of the cheese right through into the middle. At perfect ripeness, the rind mottles and you may even see white mould growing on the surface.

Storing

The easiest is probably the best, wrapped in the original wrapper in the fridge. Greaseproof or waxed paper is your next best bet – as it allows the cheese to breathe – and then pop in an airtight container and in the fridge. Plastic wrap is okay for short periods but it can cause the cheese to sweat pretty quickly.

Freezing: Don't bother trying.

When is it past it?

Ripe cheese smells mushroomy and earthy. A hint of ammonia is okay but if it's overpowering, the cheese is past its best. To make sure, let the cheese reach room temperature before making a final assessment.

Using

White mould cheeses aren't often found in cooked recipes because they can get chewy but quick cooking is fine and they're fantastic as a last-minute addition to hot dishes.

Using Up

Top Tips for White Mould Cheese

Take any combination.

- **CHICKEN, STEAK, PORK.** Drape slices of cheese over warm fillet steak, pork chops or grilled chicken and let the warmth soften the cheese. **If you have it:** Create a warm salad by adding avocado, red onion slices and honey mustard dressing.
- **PÂTÉ.** Blend 100 grams with 100 grams creamy cheese, 100 grams walnuts and 1 teaspoon cognac or port. Serve with grapes, strawberries, raisin bread and oat biscuits.
- **SAUCE.** Add cheese to plain white sauce for a dressing that seems to taste good with everything. Melt 1 tablespoon butter and add 1 tablespoon flour. Stir while cooking for 2 minutes. Stir in ½ cup milk. Bring to boil and keep stirring. Melt ½ wedge of cheese in sauce. Pour over steamed asparagus, chicken, grilled oysters, fish fillets even meatballs. **If you have it:** Add ½ teaspoon mustard or curry powder or ¼ teaspoon nutmeg.
- **STICKY DESSERT.** Place a few thick slices of cheese in the bottom of each dessert bowl and top with dried or preserved fruits and fresh fruits then drizzle with this nutty toffee: (for 4 people) melt 1 tablespoon butter in 3 cups sugar over a very low heat until it turns golden. Add 50 grams chopped nuts. Remove and pour over each serving. **If you have it:** Try walnuts with preserved ginger, dried figs and fresh apples.
- **TASTY TARTS.** Cut 1 frozen puff pastry sheet into 4, and another into 1.5-cm strips. Layer strips along edges of the squares. Bake pastry tarts in a hot oven for about 12 minutes or until the sides are puffed. Sauté 300 grams mushrooms in 1 tablespoon butter. Pour into tart and top with slices of cheese. Bake a further 5 minutes or until the pastry is golden and the cheese melts. **If you have it:** Replace mushrooms with caramelised onion or butter sautéed spinach.

Cheddar

Buying

Avoid dryness or cracks on the surface.

Variety	Maturity
Mild cheddar	1–3 months
Semi-matured	3–6 months
Matured or tasty	6–12 months
Vintage	12–24 months

Storing

Keep in the fridge in the wrapping it was sold in. Wrap in waxed or baking paper and then put in an airtight container in the fridge.

Freezing: Tends to make the cheese dry and crumbly. But if you want grated cheddar for cooking it's fine.

CONTAINED CONTENTMENT

I keep cheese in a container in the fridge. It's about 4 inches wide, 6—7 inches long and 1½ inches deep and I am in love with it! The cheese almost never goes off and it fits strange shaped cheese too.
Marjorie

When is it past it?

Harmless mould can develop on cheese, particularly cheddar. Simply cut it off. There's no hard and fast rule but obviously, if the mould is orange or black in colour, throw it out.

Using

We think you know what to do here but if you're stuck, go back to the beginning of the chapter (see p. 81) and check out Top Tips for Any Old Cheese – they work really well for cheddar.

Holey Cheese or Swiss-style – Gruyere, Emmental, Tilsit, Edam, Gouda, Raclette

Buying

Shiny eyes or holes are a good sign of a healthy cheese. So too is a smooth surface rind with no cracks. But don't worry if small cracks appear in the flesh of the cheese; that's normal.

Storing

You only need to cover the exposed surface with plastic wrap before refrigerating. This way, the rind can breathe.

Freezing: Don't bother unless you want grated cheese for cooking.

When is it past it?

Dairy Australia provides good advice on cheese mould. If the mould is orange or black in colour, the cheese should be discarded. Otherwise the mould is likely to be harmless so simply cut it off.

Using Up

Take any combination

- **FRIED.** Pile a couple of tablespoons of grated cheese onto a hot non-stick frypan. When it fries to a light golden colour on the edges, about a minute, flip. Cook for another minute on the other side. Top off salads, serve with a big breakfast.
- **FRITTATA.** Although you can make lovely frittatas with any cheese, Swiss-style melts beautifully both on top and inside this dish. Sauté 1 chopped onion and 1 crushed clove garlic in a little oil. Whisk 5 eggs with ⅓ cup grated cheese. Combine egg mixture and onions in pan. Arrange 10 thin asparagus spears on top like the spokes of a wheel and cook on low heat until almost set. Sprinkle another ⅓ cup grated cheese on the top. Grill until the cheese is bubbling. **If you have it:** Bake with 1 teaspoon thyme or tarragon.
- **GRATIN.** Holey cheeses make great gratin because they melt so well. Good too with any other hard or semi-hard cheese. Combine 4 sliced potatoes and 1–2 finely chopped onions. Layer ½ the mixture in a shallow casserole dish. Sprinkle with ½ cup grated cheese. Layer the rest of the mixture and sprinkle with another ½ cup cheese. Pour 1 cup milk over the lot. Bake for about 1 hour in a moderate oven or until the potatoes are tender. **If you have it:** Replace the potatoes with other vegies like cauliflower, celeriac or even pumpkin.
- **GRILLED CHEESE SANDWICH.** Try the Dutch version, on rye bread with thinly sliced red onion and cumin seeds. Or try cheese and thinly sliced pear.
- **TORTILLAS.** Grill or fry 2 chicken fillets and cut into strips. (Use 1 cup chopped ham if you don't have chicken.) Add 1 sliced avocado, 1 cup sweetcorn kernels, 1 cup grated cheese, ¼ cup chopped coriander, the juice of 1 lime and a good splash Tabasco. Spread mixture onto 4 tortillas. Roll tortillas like crepes and bake in moderate oven for 7–8 minutes. **If you have it:** Add chopped tomatoes.

Hard Cheese –
Pecorino, Parmesan, Pepato, Romano

Storing

Covered, in the fridge. Store in an airtight container. At a pinch you could double wrap in waxed or baking paper and then plastic. Hard cheese keeps for months, even up to a year.

Freezing: Not a good idea unless you grate the cheese and then cook with it.

Using

We think you know what to do here but if you're stuck, go back to the beginning of the chapter (see p. 81) and check out Top Tips for Any Old Cheese – they work really well for hard cheeses.

When is it past it?

Harmless mould can develop on cheese, particularly hard cheeses. Simply cut it off. There's no hard and fast rule but obviously, if the mould is orange or black in colour, throw it out.

Blue Cheese –
Danish Style Blue, Blue Brie, Gorgonzola Style Blue

Buying

Look for evenly veined cheese that's shiny and not dull or grey. The natural rind should be damp but not too sticky.

Storing

In its original wrapper. Be careful using domestic foil for wrapping blue cheese for more than two weeks as it might react with the cheese. (Cheesemakers use a special laminated foil wrap.)

Store blue cheese away from other cheeses because their mould spores can travel easily through the air and start growing where they're not wanted. Also, although blue cheese can be pretty smelly itself, it can also pick up strong odours from other foods in the fridge.

Freezing: Don't.

When is it past it?

If it's slimy, brown, or smells strongly like ammonia, throw it out. The good news is that blue cheeses contain a lot of salt that greatly reduces the chances of anything harmful growing in the short term.

Using Up

Top Tips for Blue Cheese

Take any combination

- **DRESSING.** If you don't have quite enough blue cheese for your salad, stick it in the dressing. Add 1–3 tablespoons to 1 tablespoon vinegar, 3 tablespoons oil and ¼ teaspoon Dijon mustard. Goes well over fresh beetroot and walnuts; good with coleslaw.
- **MEAT.** Crumble up to 125 grams into meatball mixture or add ¼ cup into any meat casserole or stew. Top steaks with a generous smear of cheese and a balsamic reduction: ¾ cup balsamic vinegar and 1 teaspoon sugar reduced by about half. It only takes a few minutes and perfectly complements the blue cheese and steak.
- **PUMPKIN RISOTTO.** Sauté 1 chopped onion and 1 tablespoon chopped sage in a little oil. Stir in 2 cups risotto rice to coat grains. Gradually add 5–6 cups stock and 1½ cups cubed pumpkin, boiling gently and stirring occasionally. Cook until almost all the liquid has been absorbed. Stir in 75 grams crumbled blue cheese and 40 grams toasted chopped walnuts.
- **SAUCE.** Luxurious addition to pasta or grilled chicken fillets. Heat 125 grams with 2 crushed cloves garlic, ¾ cup cream and ½ cup white wine. Cool, slowly add 2 egg yolks. Reheat without boiling. **If you have it:** Serve with ¼ cup chopped parsley and sautéed mushrooms.
- **SILVERBEET OR CABBAGE SALAD.** Blue cheese is great with strong-tasting vegetables. Also try crumbling over broccoli, cauliflower and brussel sprouts. Sauté 1 chopped onion and 2 chopped bacon rashers. Add ½ finely chopped cabbage or 1 small bunch finely chopped silverbeet and toss in the oil. Cool. Add 75 grams crumbled blue cheese combined with ⅓ cup mayonnaise. **If you have it:** Add ⅓ cup chopped hazelnuts or pine nuts and ½ cup chopped chives.

Chicken

Ideas for the remains of last night's roast

Roasting a whole chook may seem to make economic sense. But only if you have ideas for using it all up. After all, you can't stick it in the freezer – it dries up. Think of cooked chicken in the starring role for tapas, lunch or even another dinner.

Spread the news – not the germs

Lots of us wash or wipe chicken and turkey before cooking, but it's not necessary – and in fact it's probably not a good idea. Washing can spread bacteria to utensils and benchtops. Cooking is the only thing that destroys all bacteria – so get it in the pan or the oven and start cooking.

Buying

Raw: The skin and flesh should be creamy white (except for the small percentage of corn-fed chickens which have deep-yellow skin and flesh).

Don't buy fresh whole chicken to freeze. You're better off buying already frozen: the quicker it's frozen, the better it is when thawed, and commercial freezers are more efficient than domestic.

The chicks are getting bigger

It's all due to selective breeding programs – not hormones. That practice was banned in Australia more than 40 years ago. The declaration 'no added hormones' – and the labels 'produced in Australia', 'no cages' and 'grain-fed' – are superfluous as they apply to every chook sold for meat in this country. On the other hand, antibiotics are widely used. Chickens certified as free-range or organic should not have been given antibiotics at any stage during their life.

Cooked: Pick one with plump legs and breasts and look for moist, golden brown skin. If the skin is dry and taut or very dark, it's probably been too long in the rotisserie.

Storing

Raw: Both whole and pieces keep in the fridge for two or three days. Minced chicken lasts only a day. Marinating chicken should be kept in the fridge.

Cooked: Cool roasts and meals as quickly as possible. You can speed things up by dividing the chicken into portions. It keeps in fridge for three or four days in sealed containers.

Freezing

Raw: Make sure packaging is airtight, otherwise the meat will be tough. Chicken freezes up to six months.

Cooked: Chicken meals in sauce freeze for up to four months. Frozen pieces and slices tend to dry out without any sauce or liquid.

Thawing

Best to thaw in the fridge. A frozen whole chicken will take one or two days. Boneless usually defrosts overnight. Put it in a tray to catch any juices. Never thaw chicken on the kitchen counter, but you can use the microwave. Always make sure the chicken is completely thawed before cooking. Check that there are no ice crystals left in the body cavity and the legs and thighs should be soft and move easily.

Using

How much

180 grams cooked chicken = 1 cup

Thoroughly wash all surfaces and utensils in hot soapy water after working with raw chicken.

Never put cooked chicken back on the same plate that held the raw chicken. A temptation perhaps at the barbie – but asking for trouble.

Roasting tips

- A 1.5 kg whole stuffed chicken takes about 30 minutes per 500 grams in a preheated, moderate oven.
- Stick a skewer through the thickest part to check that the juices are running absolutely clear, not pink.
- Stuff just before cooking, to avoid contamination by bacteria from the raw chicken juices. Only fill cavity ⅔ full and remove immediately after cooking.
- Before cutting up, cover with foil and rest for 5–10 minutes to let the juices settle and help keep the meat moist.

DID YOU KNOW?

Each Australian now eats an average 35 kilograms of chicken a year, compared to six kilograms in the 1960s.

Using Up

A Mere Morsel

- **CHICKEN PIZZA.** Spread small pizza bases with tomato paste spiced up with some chilli sauce. Top with shredded cooked chicken, red and green capsicum, avocado and sliced mushrooms. Finish with grated cheese. Finely chopped chilli is another option if you like it hot. Pop in a moderately hot oven for about 20 minutes.
- **CREAMY CHICKEN.** Mix leftover chicken strips with a few tablespoons of mayonnaise and flavour with herbs such as chopped tarragon, mint or basil. Serve for lunch in a crusty roll, an avocado shell or on a bed of lettuce.
- **NOODLE SOUP.** Quick and easy. Cook a small chopped onion in a little chicken stock for about 5 minutes. Add more chicken stock, vermicelli noodles and shredded chicken.
- **STUFFED EGGS.** Hard boil an egg. Slice in half lengthwise. Mix egg yolk with finely chopped or minced chicken, mayonnaise and a dash of tomato sauce and spoon into the eggwhite halves. Serve on lettuce leaves.

A Leg or Two

- **CHICKEN AND CORN SOUP.** Sauté 1 chopped onion in a little oil until soft. Add 3 cups chicken stock, 2 cups shredded chicken, 310 g can creamed corn, 3 chopped spring onions. Stir until heated through. Whisk 2 eggwhites and gradually pour into the soup, stirring constantly until white ribbons swirl though the soup. Remove from heat and serve immediately.
- **CHICKEN MANGO SALAD.** Mix cooked chicken pieces with ¼ sliced, deseeded cucumber, 1 cup chopped coriander and ½ finely sliced red onion. For dressing, blend flesh of 1 mango and grated rind and juice 1 lemon. Gradually add olive oil (about ¼ cup) until the dressing is smooth. Pour dressing over salad just before serving.
- **CHICKEN NACHOS.** Make a spicy bean sauce with 1 chopped onion sautéed in a little oil, 400 g can crushed

tomatoes, a dash of hot chilli sauce and 400 g can red kidney beans. Bring to the boil and simmer for 5 minutes until sauce thickens. Add 1 cup or more chopped chicken. Layer corn chips, tomato-chicken mixture and 1 cup grated cheese. Heat in oven until cheese melts. Remove and top with guacamole (see p. 20) and sour cream. **If you have it:** Add some chopped jalapeno peppers and a few sliced black olives along with the crushed tomatoes.

- **ORANGE CHICKEN.** Blend juice and rind 2 oranges and 2 tablespoons honey with a little water or, better still, some liquid from the pan you've roasted the chicken in, and cook for a few minutes, stirring all the time. Pour sauce over chicken pieces and bake in medium hot oven for 15 minutes. Serve with rice and a green salad.

- **PESTO PASTA.** Couldn't be simpler. Add cream to basil pesto to thin it out, add 1 heaped cupful of cooked chicken, heat and toss through pasta.

- **SPICY CHICKEN BALLS.** Combine 1 heaped cup finely chopped chicken, 1 egg, 1 cup soft breadcrumbs, ¾ cup chopped coriander leaves, 3 finely chopped spring onions and 1 finely chopped chilli. Make into 8 balls and fry until golden. Serve with sweet chilli sauce for dipping.

- **STIR-FRY.** Cook 2 crushed cloves garlic and a 2-centimetre knob grated ginger in a little oil until fragrant. Add vegetables, cut into strips (e.g. red capsicum, carrot, broccoli, celery) and stir-fry until softened. Combine 2 tablespoons soy sauce and ¼ cup honey and add to vegetables. Bring to the boil and add 1–2 cups chicken pieces, ½ cup snow peas and 1 bok choy, torn into pieces. Add a 500 g packet Hokkein noodles. Heat through, adding a handful of chopped coriander at the end. **If you have it:** Cook in peanut oil.

A Little Effort

- **CHICKEN AND LEEK PIE.** You can add just about any other vegetable to this dish: mushrooms, potatoes, sweetcorn, peas, spinach, parsnips, carrots and broad beans. Melt 30 grams butter, add 2 tablespoons flour and cook, stirring for a few minutes. Whisk in 1¼ cups milk and cook over a medium heat, stirring all the time until the sauce is smooth.

Season well and add 1 tablespoon mustard. Cut chicken into cubes and leeks into thin slices and add to the sauce with 1 tablespoon each chopped chives and parsley. If you're adding other vegetables, you may have to lightly steam them first then throw into the mix. Pour into pie dish, cover with puff pastry, brushing the top with a little milk or beaten egg. Cut some steam vents. Bake in a hot oven for 20–30 minutes. Reduce heat to moderate and bake for a further 10 minutes or until pastry turns golden.

- **CURRY.** Sauté 1 large coarsely chopped onion in a little oil until nearly soft. Add 1–2 heaped tablespoons korma curry paste and cook for 1 minute until fragrant. Add 1 tablespoon tomato puree, 400 g can crushed tomatoes, 1 tablespoon vinegar and ¾ cup water. Bring to the boil and simmer uncovered for about 5 minutes. Stir in 1–2 cups cooked chicken pieces. Add 1½ cups baby spinach 1–2 minutes before serving. Garnish with coriander leaves. **If you have it:** Stir in 2 tablespoons yoghurt and juice ½ lime or lemon to taste before spinach.

STOCK RESPONSE

Chicken stock keeps in fridge 2 days or freeze in recipe portions for up to 3 months. Use for the paella recipe on the next page.

Chicken stock

Use raw or cooked carcass and leg bones. If you've used stuffing in a roast chicken, only use the leg bones. Here are the basic steps:

1. Brown chicken bones for a few minutes. **If you have it:** Use a couple of rashers of bacon to add flavour (and use the fat for browning).
2. Start with cold water covering bones, chopped vegetables and herbs. Bring slowly to the boil, remove scum from the surface, reduce heat and simmer for 2–3 hours. (Vegetables include onions, carrots, leeks, celery. Herbs and seasonings include bay leaf, parsley, thyme and peppercorns.)
3. Continually check water level and top up with hot water to keep ingredients covered.
4. Cool and strain stock, discarding bones and vegetables. Remove fat by laying a piece of paper towel over the surface and soaking it up. (Then remove the paper, of course.)

If the stock is not going to be used immediately, leave the fat to settle on the surface. When you want to use it, it's easy to lift off.

Have a go

Paella

A great all-in dish that is easier than it looks.

Ingredients

¼ teaspoon saffron
1 onion, chopped
2 cloves garlic, crushed
2 teaspoons paprika
½ cup finely chopped ham or bacon
1½ cups long grain rice
1½ pints chicken stock
¾ cup frozen peas
½ cup roasted capsicum cut into strips
2 cups cooked chicken pieces
125 grams cooked prawns
125 grams cooked white fish
Parsley

Method

Soak saffron in 2 tablespoons hot water for 20 minutes.

Sauté onion in a little oil. Add garlic, paprika, ham or bacon and rice and stir over a moderate heat until rice is transparent.

Add stock and saffron, cover and cook in moderate oven for 20 minutes.

Cook peas and add to the paella mixture. Add roasted capsicum and mix.

Toss through cooked chicken pieces, prawns and fish and return to oven for a few minutes to warm through.

Season to taste, sprinkle parsley on top and serve.

Including answers to the great Too Many Egg Yolks and Too Many Eggwhites Dilemma

Yes, we've well and truly nailed the problem of what to do with lots of whites or lots of yolks (not to mention the occasional problem of just too many eggs). And the answers are delicious.

> **People think if it's got a feather or a bit of poo on it then it's fresher but it's probably best not to eat it at all! That dirt could have gotten into the egg.**
>
> **Egg Expert**

The great freshness test

Whole: Put the egg in a pan of water. A fresh egg will sink while an old egg will float. (This doesn't tell you if the egg is bad, only old.)

Broken: The yolk of a fresh egg will be plump like a half-moon. The white will be thick and clear. In an older egg, the yolk will be flatter and more prone to breaking and spreading into the white, which will be thin and watery.

The last word: If an egg is off you'll know. Just crack it and smell it – your nose will tell you! If an egg smells or looks funny, chuck it out.

Buying

Size might matter, colour doesn't. Larger eggs have thinner shells and are more likely to crack. But the colour of an eggshell doesn't have anything to do with its quality, flavour or nutritional value. It's all down to the breed of the hen and the colour of its ear lobes!

If you buy your eggs from shops that keep them in the fridge, they'll last longer when you get them home.

It's illegal to sell eggs without a 'Best Before' date (42 days after the eggs were graded). In some states, eggs are stamped, but this is not mandatory across the country. A date on the box is fine.

Storing

Whole: Best in the main part of the fridge, in their original carton. Eggs left on the bench age seven times quicker. You can also shorten their lifespan if you use those specially designed sections in fridge doors because the eggs will be exposed to higher temperatures when the fridge is opened and closed. If you store them well, you may be able to use your eggs for several weeks after their 'Best Before' date.

Don't wash eggs, because the shell becomes even more porous when wet, making it easier for bacteria to get in.

Raw and broken: In a sealed container in the fridge for two or three days. It's the same story after you've separated the yolks and whites. To prevent the yolks from drying out, cover them with a little cold water. (Drain the water before using.)

Freezing: Don't freeze raw eggs in the shell; they might explode (as the water inside expands). Beat until just blended, then freeze in a sealed container. Substitute two tablespoons thawed egg for one fresh egg. Defrosted eggs can be used just like fresh. Your soufflés may not rise as much as with fresh but cakes and other baked goods should be fine.

Freeze eggwhites just like the whole egg. Substitute one and a half tablespoons of thawed eggwhites for one large fresh eggwhite. Thawed whites may not fluff up as much as fresh.

Egg yolks thicken or gel when they freeze, so you have to add either sugar or salt before freezing (half a teaspoon of salt or half a tablespoon of sugar for every three yolks). Substitute a half to one tablespoon of thawed yolk for one fresh yolk.

Use all frozen raw egg within three months.

Cooked: Store hard-boiled eggs in fridge and use within a week. Egg dishes can behave strangely on freezing, i.e. separate, but, in the main, freeze well. Cooked eggwhites tend to get rubbery when you freeze them.

DID YOU KNOW?

A double yolk is probably from a hormonal hen. When a hen's hormones are out of whack, she sometimes produces double-yolked eggs. The eggs are safe. But they may play havoc with your favourite sponge cake recipe.

Using

If I want to halve a recipe that uses one egg, I would halve all the other ingredients and still use a whole egg. Even with cakes and baked goods it doesn't affect the recipe. **Chef**

There's a risk of food poisoning with raw eggs, so treat them just like raw meat. (Though, luckily, our eggs come out of the chicken clean; unlike some countries, notably the US, which has a problem with *Salmonella*.)

The good news is that cooking kills any harmful microbes. But only if the food is cooked until it's hot all the way through.

So, take care when you're making recipes with raw egg, like mayonnaise, milkshakes, ice-cream, mousses and tiramisu. (Commercially available versions are generally safe and have almost certainly been made with pasteurised egg.) And after you've made these dishes, the CSIRO recommends to either serve immediately or put in the fridge.

The key to the colours of an egg

Yolk: Depends on what the hen has been eating. Wheat-based means a lemon yellow yolk. Corn or alfalfa-based gives an orange-yellow yolk.

Blood spots: These tiny red or red-brown spots are caused by the rupture of a blood vessel while the egg was being formed. Blood spots don't mean a fertilised egg. They're safe to eat.

White ropey things (chalaza): The two chalaza in the egg anchor the yolk in the centre of the white. The fresher the egg, the more noticeable they are. They're safe to eat and generally disappear in cooking.

The grey ring: This sometimes appears around the yolk of hard-boiled eggs. It's the result of a reaction between the sulphur and iron naturally found in eggs. Technically, the eggs are overcooked (but some of us actually like them this way).

Using Up

If you want to get a perfectly centred yolk for your hard-boiled eggs, just tip the carton on its side. Leave it overnight and you'll have perfect eggs every time!

Janis C

The hot and the cold

Cold eggs are easier to separate into whites and yolks. However, room temperature eggs generally cook better, so leave eggs on the bench for 30 minutes before cooking with them. They behave better in cakes and other baked goods. Also, whites whip better at room temperature.

A Glut of Ageing Eggs

Here are a couple of ideas instead of the usual omelette or frittata.

- **CHINESE EGG DROP SOUP.** Bring to boil 6 cups chicken stock (it would be worth making your own for this dish – see p. 101), ½ teaspoon grated ginger, 1½ tablespoon soy sauce and 2 tablespoons dry sherry or Chinese rice wine. Reduce to a simmer. Pour in 1 lightly beaten egg while stirring the soup. The egg will spread and feather. Bring the soup back to the boil and add another egg stirring all the while. Repeat with third egg. Turn off the heat. Add 2 chopped spring onions. **If you have it:** Add a few drops of sesame oil and some thin egg noodles a few minutes before serving.
- **JAPANESE EGG ROLL.** Much easier than you would think and so easy to vary. Heat 1 tablespoon sugar and 1 tablespoon fish sauce until the sugar dissolves. Cool. Whisk 6 eggs into the mixture. Pour ¼ of the mixture into a frypan and cook until just golden on bottom but still moist on top. Slide onto a plate. Makes 4 omelettes. For the filling, stir-fry mushrooms in garlic. Add shredded cooked chicken or duck with a few spring onions. Divide the mixture between the omelettes and roll them up. Serve with soy sauce or sweet chilli sauce.

FANCY TOUCH

Seal eggs in a container with truffles and they'll taste of truffle. It's a great way to make an expensive food go further. But beware. Eggs can absorb cheap odours too. You may not want garlicky or oniony flavoured eggs in your cakes.

- **LEFTOVER PASTA FRITTATA.** For leftover pasta, with or without sauce attached. Drizzle enough cooking oil in a frypan to coat the bottom with oil. Spread 4 cups cooked pasta out so it covers the entire pan. Heat through. Add 4 lightly beaten eggs to a couple of tablespoons of milk and ½ cup grated cheese. Pour over pasta. Cook on low heat until almost set. Brown under the griller.
- **LEMON MERINGUE PIE.** The original no-waste dessert, using yolks and whites in separate parts of the dish. It wouldn't have survived this long without also tasting wonderful. Pre-prepare a homemade base or follow instructions on packet. Combine ½ cup cornflour and ¾ cup sugar with the juice 1 lemon and 1 cup water. Simmer, uncovered, for 20 minutes, whisking occasionally. Remove from heat and stir in the rind 1 lemon, 4 egg yolks and 80 grams butter. Beat 4 eggwhites to soft peaks. Gradually beat in ½ cup sugar, a tablespoon at a time, until sugar dissolves. Spoon lemon mixture into pastry case. Top with meringue. Bake for about 8 minutes in a moderate oven or until meringue is lightly browned. Best eaten on the day, as it tends to weep.

The old and the new

Fresh eggs are ideal for poaching and frying because they hold their shape better. Older eggs are best for hard-boiling because they're easier to peel. You can use your oldest eggs for baking cakes, quiches and frittatas.

Eggwhite

- **BATTER.** Fluff up your favourite batter with whipped eggwhite, from frying fish to making pancakes.
- **COCONUT ROUGHS.** To every whipped eggwhite, add ¼ cup sugar, 1 tablespoon coconut and 20 grams shaved chocolate. Bake small teaspoons for 20–25 minutes in moderately slow oven.
- **CREAM.** Lighten up whipped cream by folding a stiff white into the mix.

- **GLAZE.** Beat lightly and brush over your pastry to make it shine. If it isn't your pastry this will make a bought one look like it is.

- **MERINGUE.** Dead easy if you obey Rule 1. Meringues are sticklers for Rule 1.

  Rule 1. Eggwhites will not whip if they come into contact with even the slightest trace of fat, grease, egg yolk or moisture. Wash and dry your hands, the beaters, the bowl and any other utensils you're using. Don't even stick your finger in the bowl to fish out a speck of egg yolk – it could add grease to the whites. Avoid using plastic bowls as they can harbour traces of fat. (Stainless steel and glass are ideal.)

  Rule 2. Eggwhites right out of the refrigerator don't whip well. (They only need 30 minutes on the benchtop.)

  Rule 3. If you make meringues on a rainy or really humid day they may fall flat.

  Rule 4. Don't add sugar before whipping. It'll increase the time it takes to get a foam. Add the sugar at the very end when you have soft peaks. Add it gradually, a few spoonfuls at a time, continuously beating. Add between 1½ and 3 tablespoons sugar per eggwhite.

  Tip: When separating eggs, use 3 bowls. 1 for the yolks. 1 for the whites. Then 1 extra bowl to break each new egg into. This way if you stuff it up and break a yolk into the white you won't have to throw out a whole batch of whites and start again.

  Fact: A beaten eggwhite can foam to 6 to 8 times its original volume.

  Second helpings: Store meringues in sealed container in cool place. Don't put them in the fridge.

- **ROYAL ICING.** The King, or Queen, of icings preferred by cake decorators. Often piped onto cakes and biscuits. It hardens when exposed to the air, so is also used to coat cakes and helps keep them moist. Wrap icing in plastic wrap if not using immediately. Whip an eggwhite into peaks with a squeeze of lemon juice (optional). Slowly whip 1½ cups icing sugar into the mix. (Also lovely but not strictly royal, is whipping in 4 tablespoons jam.)

THE PERFECT SPONGE CAKE

If you're making a special cake, don't go shaking your eggs about. Agitation can thin the whites, decreasing their cooking quality. This could be the secret to the perfect sponge!

- **SUGAR-COATED NUTS.** One eggwhite coats a little less than 500 grams nuts. Add ¾ cup sugar and dash of vanilla for every stiff eggwhite and then throw in the nuts. Spread out on oven tray for 10–15 minutes in a slow oven.
- **VELVETING.** The secret to the lovely velvety texture of Chinese food is to dip strips of chicken, meat or prawns into very lightly beaten eggwhite (don't froth it) mixed with 1 tablespoon cornflour. Refrigerate 30 minutes. Stir-fry.

Egg Yolk

- **BAKED FRUIT CUSTARD.** Brilliant way to use up ageing fruit by baking it into a gorgeous dessert. Beat two egg yolks with 1 cup cream and/or milk. Add sugar to taste and pour over your favourite stewed or fresh fruit. Bake for 30 minutes.
- **CARBONARA.** Egg yolks are the secret to sticky, silky carbonara. Combine 2–3 egg yolks, ¼ cup cream and 3 cloves minced garlic. Add to cooked hot pasta. Toss thoroughly until combined. Add 6 rashers chopped, fried bacon and ½ cup grated cheese.
- **MAYONNAISE.** Easy as pie. The trick is patience. Not hours, just minutes. Just add the drops of oil slowly. Whisk 2 yolks with 3 tablespoons lemon juice until smooth and light. Add 1 cup oil. At first, only a few drops at a time, whisking all the while. After about ⅓ cup oil you can speed up the pouring. **If you have it:** Add ½ teaspoon grainy mustard at the end.
- **PASTRY GLAZE.** A yolk beaten with a little milk gives a rich colour to sweet and savoury pies.
- **SAUCE AND SOUP THICKENER.** Yolks give a silky texture. Mix first with a little cream/milk or some of the cold soup/sauce before stirring in so it doesn't curdle.
- **SILKEN MASHED POTATOES.** Beaten into mashed potatoes makes them lovely and creamy.
- **YELLOW SPONGE CAKE.** This makes two smaller cakes that you can combine with jam and cream, or 1 large cake. Beat 6 egg yolks, ¼ cup milk and 1 cup sugar. Add 2 teaspoons vanilla. Fold in 2 cups self-raising flour and another ½ cup milk. Pour equal amounts into two 23 cm cake tins. Bake in a moderate oven for 25–35 minutes.

MERINGUE SUGGESTIONS

Pavlova: top with whipped cream and fruit.
Biscuits: fold in chocolate chips and/or nuts before cooking.
Eton Mess: crack into tall glasses and add whipped cream and fresh berries.

Have a go

Pecan Pie

Delightfully simple and tasty pie to use up yolks.

Ingredients

Sweet pastry case/frozen pastry/homemade pastry
4 egg yolks, lightly beaten
¼ cup cream
⅓ cup golden syrup
½ cup brown sugar
60 grams butter
1 teaspoon vanilla
1½ cups pecans

Method

Use a bought pastry case (or prepare a base from homemade pastry or follow instructions on pastry packet).

Combine egg yolks, cream, golden syrup, sugar and butter.

Stir over low heat until it starts to thicken, about 7 minutes. Don't boil.

Add vanilla. Stir.

Arrange pecans, top sides up, in the bottom of pastry case. Pour the filling over the nuts. Bake in moderate oven for about 20 minutes, or until the filling is puffed and golden. **If you have it:** Just as nice with walnuts or almonds. You can make a pie base from unwanted biscuits (see p. 51).

Garlic

What to do when it starts to sprout

It's been worshipped, used to ward off the undead and even exchanged as currency. But when it comes to food, garlic is generally seen as a supporting player. Can garlic be the star? You bet; it all depends on how you cook it.

Every which way you cut it

Whether you mince, crush or chop your garlic, you still have to remove the papery skin. Try the chef's trick and crush cloves with the flat blade of a large kitchen knife before peeling. Or if you've got a bunch of cloves to peel, blanch them in boiling water for 30 seconds. They will then slip out of their skins.

Buying

Look for heavy bulbs with firm, dry skin. If it's started to sprout, it's old and won't last long.

Season: All year round. Most of our garlic comes from China. The Australian product is harder to find and only available during the first half of the year.

Black garlic

It looks like mouldy garlic but it's a groovy new ingredient. It's just the white stuff fermented and aged. The inside is actually jet-black and soft. It can be spread, like cream cheese, or as one provedore put it, like Vegemite. The taste? Less pungent, with a whiff of balsamic or caramel.

Storing

Whole: In a cool, dry, dark place. Don't store garlic in the fridge. In most places in Australia garlic will last between two to four weeks. In high humidity, garlic will sprout. It's still edible but time to start cooking.

Cut: Store crushed garlic in an airtight container in the fridge for a few days.

Dried: Powdered or flaked garlic lasts up to three months in an airtight container in a cool, dry place.

Oil: In the fridge or it could spoil. That includes marinades with garlic. At room temperature, garlic can encourage the growth of the botulism toxin. For commercial garlic oils, check the label.

Freezing: Not highly recommended because garlic dries out and the flavour changes a little; primarily it's less potent. But it's a better alternative than the bin. Peel or chop and put in a sealed container. Keeps for months.

Cooked: Roasted garlic lasts a few days in an airtight container in the fridge.

Using

How much

1 medium clove = 1 teaspoon crushed
= ⅛ teaspoon powdered garlic
= ½ teaspoon bottled minced

Many recipes begin . . . 'sauté onion and garlic'. There's a reason for the order: you add the onion to the pan first as it takes longer to cook, then the garlic, preventing it from browning and becoming bitter.

Using Up

A Few Spare Sprouted

- **BUTTER.** Add to butter with parsley and chilli. Just the topping for a Scotch fillet.
- **GLAZE.** Add 2 crushed cloves to 2 tablespoons honey, 1 tablespoon Dijon mustard, 1 teaspoon sesame oil and 1 tablespoon chopped fresh ginger. Paint over pork and lamb and roast.
- **MARINADE.** All you really need is crushed garlic and oil. Brush on meat or over vegies before grilling and marinate for at least ½ hour. Particularly great on mushrooms (see p. 132, 137, 138, 143 and 150 for more marinades). **If you have it:** Add lemon juice or vinegar and chopped herbs.
- **PASTA.** Fry up garlic, chilli and breadcrumbs and toss over pasta with parsley and a little extra olive oil to coat the pasta. **If you have it:** Add lemon zest and grated parmesan.
- **PIZZA BASE.** Use marinade (above) instead of tomato paste, particularly for the white pizza (see p. 194).
- **SOUP.** Mince 1 raw clove garlic into vegetable and bean soup to give that rich Mediterranean flavour.
- **TOAST.** Rub clove over toasted bread (sourdough is perfect) before adding chopped tomato; or over toast before chopping up for croutons.
- **TOMATO SAUCE.** The purists have no onion in their sauce, only tomatoes and garlic (see p. 218).

Garlic Glut

- **GARLIC CHICKEN.** An all-in dish that gets better and better the longer you cook it. Combine in a roasting pan: 1½–2 kilograms chicken, cut into pieces around the size of a leg, juice and zest of 2 lemons, 3–4 sprigs oregano or thyme, 10 peeled cloves of garlic, ½ cup olive oil and 1 cup white wine. Mix well and spread evenly, with chicken pieces skin side up. Roast uncovered in moderate oven for 1½ hours. Halfway through cooking, baste the chicken with the juices.

- **GARLIC PRAWNS.** Fry 4 crushed cloves garlic in ¼ cup oil, with chilli to taste. Add 750 grams shelled and deveined prawns. Stir until prawns turn pink. Add 2 tablespoons lemon juice, cook for another minute or so. Toss through 2–3 tablespoons chopped parsley. Serve with crusty bread or rice. **If you have it:** Add 1 tablespoon sherry.

- **LEBANESE GARLIC SAUCE (TOUM).** Add ¼ cup lemon juice and ½ cup olive oil to a head of garlic, crushed, and a generous pinch of salt, to taste. Dollop on cooked meat and chicken.

- **ROASTED.** Roasted garlic is milder and sweeter than raw. So it's perfect for using up a glut because you can use a lot more and it tastes great. Slice off the top of the garlic bulb, just enough to barely expose the garlic inside each clove. Drizzle with oil and cover with foil. Cook in a moderate oven for about 45 minutes until the garlic is golden brown and soft. Cool and squeeze out the contents of each clove, discarding the hulls. Then there are all sorts of ways to use it.

  Spread or dip. Spread on toast as it is or make a simple dip. Blend the pulp from 1 bulb (about 15 cloves) with ½ cup oil and 1½ cups sun-dried tomatoes. Keeps for days in tightly sealed container in the fridge. Makes fantastic croutons for soup. Just smear over toast.

  Dressing. Slather over potatoes or other vegetables, with meats such as lamb, chicken, prawns – you name it.

  Soup. 5–10 minutes before you finish cooking, squeeze in an entire bulb of garlic. (See p. 45 for a roasted garlic soup.)

  Baked frittata. Combine 1 head garlic, roasted until it has just softened, (pop the individual cloves into mixing bowl) with 6 lightly beaten eggs, 1 cup grated parmesan and ⅓ cup chopped parsley. Spoon into a baking dish and cook in moderate oven for 40–45 minutes or until puffed and golden.

Herbs

How to enjoy your herbs again and again

Fresh herbs can really make a dish. Often though, you're left with a whole lotta leaves that quickly go brown and slimy in the crisper. And you're likely to end up throwing away the very herb that could make your next meal absolutely fabulous.

Iced herbs

With a little effort you can make your herbs last up to six months. Chop them into ice-cube trays with a little water. When they're frozen, you can pop them out into an airtight container. If you measure 1 tablespoon of chopped herbs into every cube, following recipes will be a doddle.

WASTE WARRIOR TIP

The easiest way to save herbs is to freeze them. Just drop into an airtight container. You don't even need to chop herbs like dill, oregano, rosemary and thyme: just stick the whole sprigs into a plastic bag and throw into the freezer.

Substitutions

1 tablespoon basil	= 1 tablespoon mint (for both sweet and savoury dishes)
1 tablespoon chives	= 1 tablespoon green tops from spring onions
	= 1 tablespoon garlic chives
	= 1 tablespoon Chinese garlic stems
1 tablespoon coriander	= there isn't a good alternative but for a garnish you can try flat leaf parsley
1 tablespoon dill	= 1 tablespoon tarragon in fish and egg dishes
(1 tablespoon dill as a garnish	= 1 tablespoon fennel leaves – it looks very similar)
1 tablespoon oregano	= 2 tablespoons marjoram
1 tablespoon parsley	= 1 tablespoon chervil
1 tablespoon rosemary	= 1 tablespoon thyme/tarragon/savory
1 tablespoon sage	= 1 tablespoon savory/rosemary or 2 tablespoons marjoram
1 tablespoon tarragon	= 1 tablespoon chervil or 1 teaspoon fennel seed
1 tablespoon thyme	= 1 tablespoon basil/oregano/savory

Seven Sensational Herb Help Hints

1. **Artistic Licence.** If you don't have the herb listed in a recipe, try another herb, or a combination. You'll be surprised at how often the resulting dish is a success.
2. **Breadcrumbs.** Take leftover herbs and stale bread and create a gourmet dish. As a ballpark figure, for every cup breadcrumbs add ½ cup chives/parsley/basil or 2 tablespoons thyme/oregano or 1 tablespoon rosemary/sage/tarragon. Best to make as needed as the herby breadcrumbs don't keep for long. Dip veal, chicken or fish fillets into seasoned flour, then whisked egg (or milk if you don't have eggs) and finally, herb breadcrumbs. Rest in fridge 30 minutes. Shallow fry.
3. **Butter.** Use herb butter in omelettes, to finish risotto or spread on just-cooked steaks, fish fillets or vegetables. It also freezes well. Blend butter with chopped herbs. Wrap in plastic or waxed wrap (or put it back in the butter container) and chill. Use 4 tablespoons chopped herbs for 125 grams butter.
4. **Olive oil.** Herb-infused olive oil adds effortless flavour to cooking as well as salads and marinades. Wash and dry herbs well before covering in oil and refrigerate.
5. **Roasted.** The beauty of roasting herbs with vegetables is that you don't have to chop: just throw the sprigs in with the oil. That also means you'll use up quite a bit. Oregano, parsley, rosemary, thyme, tarragon and sage love potatoes. But don't stop there. Try with pumpkin, sweet potato, squash, carrots, beetroot, whole onions and heads of garlic.
6. **Steamed/Baked.** Give a fragrant flavour to steamed fish with great handfuls of herbs. Try coriander, mint, dill, parsley and chives. Put fish fillets on a sheet of oiled baking paper which is on a sheet of foil. Cover each fillet with mixture of a handful of chopped onions, 1 cup chopped herbs, a couple of slices lemon and a splash of oil. Fold foil edges inwards to form sealed bag. Bake for 15–20 minutes or until fish is cooked through.
7. **Vinegar.** Herb-infused vinegar provides instant flavour for salad dressings and marinades. Wash and dry the herbs well before you throw into a jar or bottle and cover with vinegar. Secure tightly and store in a cool, dry place. Lasts for at least a month.

SUBSTITUTING FRESH FOR DRIED

1 teaspoon dried herb = 1 tablespoon fresh herb

STORE WARNING

Don't store herb-infused olive oil out of the fridge, as it is not a preservative and may actually promote the growth of some types of bacteria.

Basil

Buying

Common (or green) basil and Thai basil (purplish stems and thinner leaves) can be used interchangeably in most recipes, especially when cooked.

Season: Tends to be cheaper and better quality in summer.

Storing

TO CUT OR NOT TO CUT

Some chefs swear that it is better to tear basil leaves as cutting reduces its intense flavour. We can't tell the difference.

Bunch: Basil looks robust but it can be a bit of a goldilocks; it doesn't like to be too hot, too cold, too dry or too wet. Wrap in a dry paper towel in a sealed plastic bag, plastic wrap or airtight container. Store in a cool spot or in a warmer section of the fridge as it is susceptible to chilling. Basil keeps for up to a week.

Freezing: Good, without affecting flavour, but only for cooked dishes.

Using

Basil has a deeper flavour when cooked but it's also lovely eaten raw. So, you can add it at the beginning of cooking or a minute or two before serving.

Using Up

- **BEEF STIR-FRY.** Make a paste of 10–12 cloves garlic and sliced red chillies (to taste) and fry this for 20 seconds before adding ½ kilogram thinly sliced beef. Cook until most of the meat has changed colour, add 2 finely sliced red capsicums and 1 tablespoon oyster sauce, 1 tablespoon soy sauce and 1 teaspoon fish sauce. Then add 3–4 chopped spring onions and 2–3 tablespoons chicken stock and cook meat. Turn off heat. Add 1½ cups chopped basil and serve with rice.

- **CREAMY CHICKEN SALAD.** Poach 3 chicken breast fillets (approx 15 minutes in water). Add to ⅓ cup chopped basil, ½ cup sour cream, 4 finely chopped spring onions and 4 handfuls of leafy greens, such as rocket, baby spinach or lettuce.
- **EGGPLANT.** Loves basil. Blend 5–6 large leaves with a couple of tablespoons of olive oil and 50 mL white wine and brush over slices of eggplant before roasting.
- **GREEN BEANS.** A spicy oil-free dressing for just-cooked green beans. Combine ½ cup basil, 2 chopped cloves garlic, 2 chopped anchovies, ⅓ cup tomato juice, ½ teaspoon Tabasco, 2 teaspoons Worcestershire sauce.
- **PEACHES.** Basil spices up most stone fruit. Dissolve 2 cups caster sugar in 4 cups water with 2 cinnamon sticks. Add 4–5 peaches and simmer, uncovered, for 15 minutes or until the peaches are tender. Remove from heat and add ½ cup chopped basil. When cool, peel the skins from the peaches and remove stones. Chill before serving.
- **PEANUT SAUCE.** A great Thai sauce for noodles and grilled chicken, or cabbage and bean sprout-based salads. Combine 2 tablespoons peanut paste, 2 tablespoons oil, 2½ tablespoons rice wine vinegar, 1 tablespoon soy sauce, 1 chopped clove garlic, ½–1 chilli and ⅓ cup chopped basil. Makes 1 cup.
- **SALMON MAYONNAISE.** Add ⅓ cup chopped basil to ½ cup mayonnaise and ½ cup sour cream or plain yoghurt and 1 sliced spring onion. Makes enough for 4 serves of salmon.
- **STRAWBERRIES.** Basil and balsamic actually make strawberries taste more like strawberries. To about ½ kilogram halved strawberries, add 2 tablespoons sugar and 1 tablespoon balsamic vinegar. Toss and let sit for ½ hour. Add 2 tablespoons finely sliced basil leaves before serving.
- **TOMATOES.** Add 1 teaspoon basil for every serve of tomato-based sauce or soup. Try roasted tomatoes: bake halved tomatoes with a sprinkle of sugar and balsamic vinegar until soft and browned. Serve with liberal amounts of shredded basil and goat's cheese or crumbled fetta.
- **ZUCCHINI.** When you're cooking with zucchini, think basil. Add ¼ cup to zucchini slice (see p. 225). Or ½ bunch for every 6–8 serves of soup.

HERB PARTNERS

Basil works well with chives, coriander, mint, rosemary and thyme.

PESTO PIZZAZZ

It's an oldie but a goodie and pesto is still one of the best ways to use up half a bunch of basil. Blend with 1–2 cloves garlic, ½ cup grated parmesan and ¼ cup olive oil. Spread on prawns, stuff in tomatoes, stir through scrambled eggs or pasta. Freezes well.

Chives

FANCY TOUCH

Drape a long strand of chives across a dish for dramatic effect. And if you want to go crazy, use the strands to tie up bundles of green beans.

Buying

Garlic chives are wider and flatter than ordinary chives and taste just as they sound. If you are happy to have the added bonus of a strong garlicky flavour, then the two are pretty interchangeable in recipes.

Storing

Bunch: In damp paper towel in sealed plastic bag, plastic wrap or airtight container in the fridge. Ordinary chives keep for a few days but garlic chives are much more robust and keep a week or longer.

Freezing: Good, without affecting flavour but only for cooked dishes.

GARNISH WITH FLAVOUR

Don't forget that you can snip chives over all kinds of dishes. Chop a teaspoon per serving into seafood chowder, salsa, scrambled eggs, potato salad, mashed pumpkin, quiche, frittata, sandwich spread or vinaigrette dressing. Or sprinkle a teaspoon onto barbecued mushrooms, fresh oysters, cream cheese spread, asparagus or just-cooked seafood and meat.

Using

Chives lose their flavour if cooked for any length of time, so add a minute or two before serving.

Using Up

- **ANY BEAN SALAD.** Add ¼ cup chives to a punnet of halved and lightly grilled cherry tomatoes, 2 tablespoons chopped olives and 3 cups cooked beans, white, black and green. Throw over a dressing of 3 tablespoons olive oil, 1 tablespoon white wine vinegar and 1 teaspoon grainy mustard. Serve with lamb.

- **DANISH REMOULADE.** A Danish seafood sauce for hot and cold salads. Add 1 cup chopped chives to 1 cup mayonnaise, 50 grams sweet spiced gherkins, 2 tablespoons chopped capers and 1 teaspoon grainy mustard.
- **FRITTERS.** Give a subtle lift to the mild flavour of potato fritters. Add ¼ cup chopped chives to 4 potatoes, grated, 1 egg, 1 tablespoon flour, 1 tablespoon milk and 2 tablespoons grated cheese. Mix well. Shape into fritters and fry each side until golden.
- **HERB CHEESE.** Roll 150 grams creamy cheese (try goat's) in mixture of 3 tablespoons chopped chives and ⅓ cup chopped walnuts. Chill for 1–2 hours before serving.
- **MUFFINS.** Add ¼ cup chopped chives to 1 cup self-raising flour, 1 egg, ½ cup milk and 80 grams melted and cooled butter. If the batter appears dry, add a bit more milk but don't overmix. Bake in hot oven for 20–25 minutes, until the tops spring back when touched.
- **PASTA.** Make a simple but tasty dressing with ½ bunch chives, zest 1 lemon, chilli to taste, a few tablespoons of olive oil, ¼ cup soy sauce and ½ cup chicken stock. Toss just-cooked pasta in the mixture.
- **RISOTTO CAKES.** Whisk together ⅓ cup chopped chives, ½ cup yoghurt, 2 eggs, and 1½ cups Gruyere cheese. Add 1 cup cold cooked rice. Make into balls, about 5 centimetres in diameter. Cover with plastic wrap and refrigerate for at least 2 hours, until firm. Roll in breadcrumbs and fry for a couple of minutes on each side until crisp and browned.
- **ROAST BEEF SAUCE.** Add a couple of chopped tablespoons to 1 cup sour cream or yoghurt, ½ teaspoon grainy mustard and ¼ cup horseradish.
- **TZATZIKI.** Add 3 tablespoons chopped chives (or replace a tablespoon or two with dill/parsley/mint) to 1 cup plain yoghurt, 2 medium continental cucumbers, deseeded and grated, and 1 clove minced garlic. Serve as a side salad for souvlaki, a filler for baked potatoes, even a sauce for fish fingers.

HERB PARTNERS

Chives work well with basil and tarragon.

Coriander

Buying

Don't get it mixed up with flat leaf parsley, which looks very similar but tastes completely different.

WASTE WARRIOR TIP

Don't throw any of that coriander away. You can use the whole bunch. The stems can be chopped and used in the same way as the leaves. The roots have a stronger flavour and are delicious pounded into a curry paste or simmered in stock.

Storing

Bunch: In damp paper towel in sealed plastic bag, plastic wrap or airtight container in the fridge. Coriander keeps for up to five days.

Freezing: Good but only for cooked dishes.

Using

Coriander seeds have a completely different flavour to the leaves. Seeds have a mild, sweet taste and are best dry-fried to release the flavour.

Using Up

- **AVOCADO.** Coriander loves avocado. Throw them together in a salad. Try chunks of avocado, mango and cooked prawns. Add ¼–½ bunch each mint and coriander. Dress with 1 tablespoon each sugar, fish sauce and sweet chilli sauce and ⅓ cup each oil and lime juice.
- **CABBAGE.** For a simple but different Mexican-style coleslaw, add 1 cup chopped coriander to 6 cups shredded cabbage. Dress with ¼ cup each lime juice and oil, 1 tablespoon honey and ½ teaspoon cumin.
- **INDIAN CHUTNEY.** Process ½ bunch coriander, 2 cloves garlic, 2-centimetre knob ginger, chilli (to taste), ½ teaspoon sugar and 1 teaspoon lime juice. Serve with samosas or lamb cutlets.

- **LIME RICE.** Sauté 2 crushed cloves garlic in a little oil and add 1 cup rice. Cook for few minutes, stirring frequently. Add 1½ cups chicken stock, 2 tablespoons lime juice and simmer until rice is cooked, about 15 minutes. Stir in ½ cup coriander. Side dish to Mexican or Asian dishes.
- **MIDDLE EASTERN LENTILS.** Sauté a couple of crushed cloves garlic in a little oil, add 1–2 cups cooked lentils, and dress with ¼ cup coriander and ¼ cup lemon juice. Serve hot with pita bread or cold as a salad.
- **MUSSELS.** Sauté 3 crushed cloves garlic in 2 tablespoons oil. Add 1 stick finely chopped lemongrass and 1 diced onion, ½–1 cup stock, wine or water, chilli to taste and simmer for 15 minutes. Add 1½ kilograms scrubbed mussels and ½ cup coriander. Cover and simmer for 5 minutes or until the shells open. Serve with extra coriander.
- **ORANGE FISH.** Sauté 1 sliced onion and 1 crushed clove garlic in a little oil until soft. Pour in ⅓ cup orange juice and poach 4 white fish fillets until flaky, about 20 minutes. Just before serving add ⅓ cup coriander. Also makes a great marinade for chicken, try blending ½ cup coriander, the zest and juice 1 orange, 2 teaspoons oregano and ½ cup oil.
- **PEA SOUP.** The ultimate green soup. Sauté an onion in a little oil with a few crushed cloves garlic and chilli to taste. Add 450 grams peas and 3–4 cups vegetable stock. Once the peas are soft add ⅓–½ cup coriander and puree. And don't forget to add to carrot soup (see p. 66).
- **THAI CHICKEN CURRY.** Put the green in green chicken curry. Chop then blend 1 stalk lemongrass, 2 spring onions, fresh green chillies (to taste), 2 cloves garlic, 3-centimetre knob ginger and ½ bunch coriander. Add 2 tablespoons soy sauce, 1–2 teaspoons fish sauce and ½ teaspoon sugar to make a paste. Fry for a few minutes and add 1 cup coconut milk and 1 cup chicken stock. Poach strips of chicken, red capsicum and snap peas in the liquid. Sprinkle coriander and/or basil to serve.
- **TOMATOES.** Coriander turns tomatoes into salsa. Add ½ bunch to 2 chopped ripe tomatoes, ½ red chopped onion and chilli. Dress with 2 tablespoons each oil and lemon juice. Serve on hamburgers, with curries or barbecued fish.

HERB PARTNERS

Coriander leaves work well with basil, mint, lemongrass, Kaffir lime leaves, ginger, oregano, nutmeg and cumin.

Dill

Storing

Bunch: Wrap in damp paper towel in sealed plastic bag, plastic wrap or airtight container in the fridge. Dill keeps for up to three days.

Freezing: Good. Freeze on the stalk and snip off what you need.

Using

Dill loses its flavour if cooked for any length of time, so add a minute or two before serving.

Using Up

- **ASPARAGUS.** For a fabulous warm salad add 2 tablespoons to 2 bunches steamed asparagus, 1 avocado, ¼ cup pine nuts, 2 tablespoons olive oil and 2 tablespoons lemon/lime juice.
- **CHICKEN.** Roast a chicken with a lemon and a few sprigs of dill in the cavity. Rub dill and butter under the skin.
- **DRESSING.** Dill transforms any creamy sauce. The Americans love their Ranch Dressing. Try adding ¼ cup dill to ¾ cup sour cream, 1 crushed clove garlic and 1 tablespoon grainy mustard. Throw over fish, chicken, avocado and beetroot salads.
- **EGGS.** For an American egg salad sandwich, combine 1–2 teaspoons chopped dill for each hard-boiled egg, along with 1 tablespoon mayonnaise, ½–1 teaspoon mustard, 1 teaspoon chopped spring onions and 1 tablespoon chopped cucumber.
- **FISH COOKING SAUCE.** Spread a mixture of 2 tablespoons dill, 1 tablespoon butter, 4 tablespoons chopped almonds and 2 teaspoons lemon rind on 4 white fish fillets. Bake in a hot oven 15 minutes or until cooked through.

- **GRAVLAX.** Scandinavian-style cured salmon that is more delicately flavoured than smoked. Cover raw salmon fillets with a mixture made from equal amounts of chopped dill, caster sugar and salt. Sprinkle liberally with pepper. Stack one on top of the other, mixture sandwiched inside, and wrap in plastic wrap. Cure in the fridge for 24 hours, turning stack once, so both sides are evenly cured. Brush off mixture with paper towel. Sprinkle with dill and serve finely sliced. For lemon-cured fish see ceviche (see p. 150).
- **GREEK MEAT.** Transform your steak or lamb kebab. Spread ½ cup yoghurt, 2 teaspoons chopped dill and 1 minced clove garlic onto the cooked meat.
- **QUICK PICKLES.** Instant sweet spiced pickles that keep for weeks in the fridge. Dissolve ¼ cup sugar in 1 cup white wine vinegar. Pour over 3 thinly sliced cucumbers and 4 tablespoons dill. Store in a sealed container in the fridge for a few days to let the flavour develop.
- **SALMON PATTIES.** Combine ⅓ cup chopped dill with 2 x 210 g tins salmon, 1 cup breadcrumbs, 3 sliced spring onions, zest and juice 1 lemon and 1 lightly beaten egg. Form into patties and roll in breadcrumbs. Refrigerate for ½ hour and shallow fry until golden. Serve with **dill tartare sauce:** 1 cup mayonnaise and 2 finely chopped gherkins, 1 tablespoon capers and 1 tablespoon dill.
- **TOMATO JUICE OR BLOODY MARY.** Add a sprig to a jug for a subtle richness and a wonderful bouquet.

HERB PARTNERS

Try chives, parsley and tarragon with dill.

Mint

Buying

There are lots of different varieties and they may not be interchangeable in recipes. For example, Vietnamese mint is very different to common mint. It has dark green to purple elongated leaves with pointy tips and has a hotter, more peppery flavour.

Storing

Bunch: Wrap in damp paper towel in sealed plastic bag, plastic wrap or airtight container in the fridge. Alternatively, store in a glass of water in the fridge. If you change the water daily it seems to last longer. Mint keeps for up to a week.

Freezing: Good, without flavour loss.

FANCY TOUCH

For the ultimate edible decoration, candy your mint leaves. Paint leaves with lightly beaten eggwhite and dip in caster sugar. Dry on baking paper in the fridge for at least one hour or up to three days. Use to top off a bowl of fruit or a cake.

Using

Mint loses its flavour if cooked for any length of time, so add a minute or two before serving.

Using Up

- **COCKTAILS.** Mint makes memorable cocktails, and they use a lot of it; about 10 leaves for each drink. For a Mojito, crush leaves into glass, add 1–2 shots white rum and 2 teaspoons sugar dissolved in 1 tablespoon lime juice. Top up with soda water. For a mint julep, add 1–2 shots bourbon to the crushed mint along with 1 heaped teaspoon sugar and a dash of water. Top with soda water. For brandy julep, replace the bourbon with brandy. Or try vodka and replace soda water with lemonade. Or just vodka!
- **FRESH MINT BROWNIES.** Melt 150 grams butter with 125 grams chocolate over low heat stirring constantly. Once

melted remove from heat and stir in ½ cup finely chopped mint and 2 tablespoons water. Let cool for 10 minutes and then strain out mint. Add 2 cups sugar, 4 eggs and 1½ cups self-raising flour. Pour into shallow baking pan. Bake in moderately hot oven for 45 minutes, or until the top is no longer shiny and a thin crust appears. Makes about 16 brownies.

- **FRUIT.** Mint adds zing to most fruit salads. Shred a few leaves into the bowl ½ hour before serving. Or try strawberries and watermelon. Dissolve ½ cup sugar in ¼ cup water. Add 1 punnet strawberries, halved, and the same amount of cubed watermelon. Stir in ¼ cup mint leaves. Refrigerate for at least 2 hours.
- **GREEN BEANS.** Sauté 2 chopped onions in a little oil with a couple of crushed cloves garlic. Add ½ teaspoon cinnamon and 2 tablespoons chopped mint and cook for a few minutes. Add 1 cup tinned tomatoes and ½ kilogram coarsely chopped green beans, ½ cup of chicken stock and sugar to taste. Simmer until beans are just soft.
- **INDIAN CHICKEN CURRY.** Puree ½ bunch mint leaves, 1 clove garlic, 2-centimetre knob ginger and chilli to taste. Fry with 1 chopped onion and 1 teaspoon garam masala and 1 teaspoon paprika. Add chicken pieces, cover and cook slowly, adding water when needed. Serve with rice.
- **LAMB CHOPS.** Marinate in mixture of ¼ cup chopped mint, 3 tablespoons grainy mustard, 2 tablespoons olive oil and 1 tablespoon honey. Cover and refrigerate for 4 hours. BBQ, roast or grill.
- **LEFTOVER CHICKEN PASTA.** To cooked pasta, add 1 cup mint leaves, ½ cup chives, 2 crushed cloves garlic, zest of 1 lemon and 2 tablespoons juice, ¼ cup olive oil and 2 cups shredded chicken. Eat hot or cold.
- **PEAS.** Add half a dozen finely chopped leaves to the cooking water while you boil peas. Once cooked, drain and splash with olive oil. Mash roughly and spread on toasted sourdough bread. **If you have it:** Add a smear of cream cheese or goat's cheese.
- **PESTO.** Many herbs make great pesto sauce. Mint is particularly good with lamb, potatoes and carrots. Process 1 cup mint with ¼ cup walnuts, juice of ½ a lemon and ¼ cup oil.

HERB PARTNERS

Mint is particularly popular. It works well with parsley, basil, garlic, ginger, lavender, rosemary, sage, thyme, and marjoram.

TEA TIME

Half a bunch of mint makes about three cups of tea. Soak in boiling water and steep for at least 3 minutes. Serve immediately or let cool and drink with ice.

Oregano

Buying

Check that the leaves are still attached to the stems. It's a sign of freshness.

Storing

Bunch: Wrap in damp paper towel in sealed plastic bag, plastic wrap or airtight container in the fridge. Oregano keeps for up to three days.

Freezing: Good. Freeze on the stalk and snip off what you need.

HERB PARTNERS

Oregano works well with basil, parsley, chives, thyme and bay leaves.

Using

Can be added at the beginning of cooking or a minute or two before serving.

Using Up

- **CHICKEN WITH OLIVES AND LEMON.** Sauté a couple of cloves of garlic in a little oil and brown 4–6 chicken pieces. Add 2 tablespoons oregano, 1 cup white wine, 2 cups stock, 1 cup olives and 1 lemon cut into wedges. Cover and slow cook for at least an hour. Or for fast flavour, stick a few sprigs of oregano under the skin of a whole chicken or chicken pieces before roasting.
- **LAMB MARINADE.** Combine 3 crushed cloves garlic, 3 tablespoons oregano, 2 tablespoons oil and 2 tablespoons lemon juice. Baste leg of lamb and refrigerate for 4–6 hours.
- **MEDITERRANEAN BEEF STEW.** When you have oregano, you don't need any other flavouring. Sauté 2–3

onions in a little oil, add ¾ kilogram cubed beef and brown meat. Add 3 tomatoes (tinned is fine) and 2 tablespoons oregano. Bake or simmer for about 2 hours. Add 4 cubed raw potatoes 30 minutes before the end.

- **PASTA PESTO.** Stronger in flavour than basil pesto but just as versatile. Process 1 cup oregano with 1 cup pine nuts and 1 head roasted garlic. (Cut tops off cloves and throw whole head in oven for 20 minutes. Then squeeze middle out of individual cloves.) Slowly drizzle in a good quality olive oil until it reaches a consistency you like. Stir though pasta with parmesan or spread over warm fish.
- **ROASTED VEGETABLE SALAD.** Add 1 tablespoon chopped oregano to ½ cup olive oil, 2 tablespoons white wine vinegar and 2 cloves minced garlic. Brush bite-sized pieces of pumpkin, zucchini, capsicum, red onion and eggplant and roast or barbecue. When softened, toss through 150 grams fetta cheese and 1 tablespoon toasted pine nuts. Drizzle with remaining oregano dressing.
- **SARDINES.** Make a robust sauce for strong-tasting fish. Combine 3 tablespoons oregano, 3 minced cloves garlic, 2 diced onions, a dozen or so semidried tomatoes, 2 tablespoons tomato paste and ⅓ cup white wine. Simmer fish in mixture until tender. If cooking a whole fish, throw a few sprigs into the cavity.
- **SCONES.** Rub 1–2 tablespoons butter into 1½ cups self-raising flour. Add ¼ cup finely chopped oregano and 2 tablespoons grated cheese. Roll out onto floured surface and cut into scones. Bake in very hot oven for 12 minutes or until golden. Makes 5–10 scones.
- **TOMATOES.** Throw in 2 tablespoons oregano for every cup of tomatoes you're using in any sauce or casserole. Oregano is also one of the original pizza ingredients, so you don't need too much more. Spread tomato sauce over a large pizza base, sprinkle over 3–4 tablespoons oregano leaves and top with ¼ cup grated mozzarella and parmesan.
- **WHITE BEAN DIP.** Blend 2 tablespoons with 1 can white beans (e.g. cannellini), 3 cloves crushed garlic, 2 tablespoons lemon juice, ¼ cup olive oil. Serve with fresh vegetables, crackers or toasted flat bread.

EARTHY MATCH

Mushrooms and the earthy flavours of oregano complement each other. Add 1 tablespoon for every cup of cooked mushrooms.

Parsley

Buying

Flat leaf or curly, they are treated the same in recipes. The flat leaf parsley has a stronger flavour so you will notice the difference when you use a lot of it, for example, in salads. Curly is much easier to cut.

Storing

Bunch: Wrap in damp paper towel in sealed plastic bag, plastic wrap or airtight container in the fridge. Keeps for up to five days. Alternatively, stand upright in a container with a few centimetres of water in the fridge. Cover with a plastic bag and secure with an elastic band. If you change the water daily it seems to last longer.

Freezing: Good, without affecting flavour but it doesn't really bounce back for salads.

STEMS FOR STOCK

Don't throw away those stems. They may be a bit chewy but they have a much stronger flavour than the leaves, so they're great in homemade stock. This way every dish you make from the stock has that lovely parsley flavour.

Using

Parsley loses its flavour if cooked for any length of time, so add a minute or two before serving.

Using Up

- **FISH.** Sauté 1 chopped onion in a little oil, add 1 crushed clove garlic and then add 4–8 small fillets white fish, 1–2 cups white wine, 1 cup chopped parsley and a 400 g can tomatoes. Simmer until fish is cooked through. Or sprinkle chopped parsley over grilled fish during the last minute of cooking.
- **MUSSELS.** Sauté 3 crushed cloves garlic in 2 tablespoons oil. Add 400 g can tomatoes (or 4–5 chopped fresh ones) and a little

chilli and simmer for 15 minutes. Add 1½ kilograms mussels and 4 tablespoons parsley and ½ cup stock, wine or water. Cover and simmer for 5 minutes or until the shells open.

- **PARSLEY SOUP.** Sauté 1 chopped leek and 3 crushed cloves garlic in a little oil. Add 2 celery sticks, 1 large potato, chopped, and 3 cups chicken stock. When the vegetables are soft, add 1 cup parsley leaves. Puree and reheat, adding 1 tablespoon cream.
- **PASTA WITH SUN-DRIED TOMATOES.** Puree 1 cup parsley, ½ cup sun-dried tomatoes, 1 clove garlic, 1 teaspoon lemon juice and ¼ cup olive oil. Stir through cooked hot pasta and sprinkle with parmesan.
- **PERSILLADE.** A simple parsley topping that gives a flavour hit to mushrooms, lamb chops, roasted cauliflower and steamed carrots – as well as stews and casseroles. Finely chop 3 tablespoons chopped parsley and 1 clove garlic or 1 teaspoon onion. Sprinkle just before serving. **If you have it:** Add 1 teaspoon lemon, lime or orange zest to create **GREMOLATA**. It puts zing into osso bucco, grilled fish fillets, mussels, prawns, roast chicken and lamb. Sprinkle just before serving.
- **SALAD.** Make parsley the star rather than the support act. For 2 cups parsley, add ½ minced red onion, 2 chopped tomatoes, ¼ cup black olives and 3 tablespoons capers. Dress with ¼ cup each olive oil and lemon juice. Serve with crumbled fetta cheese.
- **SALSA VERDE.** This green sauce adds a great flavour punch to seafood, chicken and vegies. And it takes a full cup of chopped parsley (see p. 36).
- **TABOULI WITH TAHINI DRESSING.** A tasty twist on tabouli that takes the edge off the bitterness of the parsley. Cover ½ cup burghul with boiling water for 10 minutes. Drain. Add 1 cup chopped parsley, 1 cup chopped mint, 1 diced tomato, 2 chopped spring onions and ½ diced Lebanese cucumber. Dress with ¼ cup tahini, ½ cup water and ½ cup lemon juice.

HERB PARTNERS

Parsley is the most gregarious of herbs, and partners with pretty much every other herb imaginable.

Rosemary

Buying

If the leaves don't bend under your fingers, then the rosemary has begun to dry out.

Storing

Bunch: In a sealed plastic bag, plastic wrap or sealed container in the fridge. Rosemary keeps for up to a week.

Freezing: Okay but it loses some of its piquancy. Freeze on the stalk and snip off what you need.

Using

Best added in the last 30 minutes of cooking.

Using Up

- **BARBECUE.** The easiest way to use up rosemary, particularly if you have your own bush, is on the barbie. Toss a few sprigs on barbeque coals to flavour the smoke. Dip sprigs in oil and baste barbecue meat and vegetables. Strip the thicker sprigs, soak in water and use as skewers for lamb, beef, prawns and vegetables.
- **BISCUITS.** Combine 1 tablespoon finely chopped rosemary, 100 grams butter, 1 cup grated cheese, ¾ cup plain flour, and a good pinch of cayenne pepper. Roll into a log and wrap in plastic wrap. Refrigerate at least 30 minutes. Slice and bake in moderate oven for 10–15 minutes, or until golden brown.
- **CHICKEN AND TOMATO.** All you need is a tablespoon to flavour the entire dish. Brown 4 pieces chicken. Sauté 1 chopped onion in a little oil, add 2–3 crushed cloves garlic

HERB PARTNERS

Rosemary likes basil, marjoram, oregano, parsley, sage, savory and thyme.

and 1 finely chopped tablespoon rosemary. Add 4–5 chopped tomatoes (or 400 g can) and about ⅓ cup red wine. Return the chicken to the pan and simmer until cooked.

- **FRITTATA.** Rosemary benefits from a little cooking time, so this is quite a clever dish. Caramelise 3 chopped onions with 1 tablespoon rosemary i.e. cook slowly until they are brown and soft. Add 8 lightly beaten eggs and a couple of tablespoons of parmesan. Cook on low heat until almost set. Brown under the grill.
- **MARINADE.** You don't have to get fancy. Add 1 tablespoon chopped rosemary to ¼ cup oil, 2 cloves chopped garlic and juice ½ lemon. Marinate zucchini, artichokes, chicken, fish, pork or lamb.
- **MUSHROOMS.** Throw 1 finely chopped teaspoon in with every 500 grams mushrooms (25 button) along with 2 crushed cloves garlic, 1 chopped slice bacon and a splash of white wine.
- **OLIVES.** For an unusual but easy snack, fry olives in 1 crushed clove garlic and 1 teaspoon chopped rosemary.
- **PEACH CHAMPAGNE.** Rosemary gives an earthy perfume to stone fruits. Simmer 3 sprigs with 4 de-stoned peaches in ½ cup sugar and 1½ cups water until the sugar dissolves. Discard the rosemary and remove the skins from the peaches. Let the liquid cool. Add to champagne or soda water.
- **POACHED PEARS.** Add a sprig to 2 cups water (or red wine), along with ⅓ cup sugar and juice 1 lemon. Add 4 peeled pears with stem intact. Lightly simmer, turning occasionally for about 1 hour. Discard the sprig before serving.
- **PORK.** Make a paste from 3 tablespoons chopped rosemary, 8 cloves garlic and 3 tablespoons fennel seeds. Rub flesh before baking.
- **SAUSAGES.** Roast 6 sausages, 4–5 potatoes, 4 cloves garlic and 2 stalks rosemary in a little oil for 30–40 minutes, stirring occasionally. Serve with fresh parsley.
- **STEAK.** Throw 1 tablespoon each chopped rosemary, oregano and sage into the cooking juices when cooking steak.

WHEN OILS AIN'T OILS

Don't drink essential, distilled rosemary oil. In strong doses, it's poisonous. It's completely different to rosemary-flavoured cooking oils – they're delicious.

Sage

Buying

New varieties are becoming more widely available and don't always substitute for each other. For example, pineapple sage tastes just as it sounds – it may not work with rabbit, but it's lovely in fruit salad and punch.

Storing

Bunch: Wrap in damp paper towel in sealed plastic bag, plastic wrap or airtight container in the fridge. Sage keeps for up to four or five days.

Freezing: Good, freeze on the stalk and snip off what you need.

Using

Heat mellows sage, so for the strongest flavour add near the end of cooking.

Using Up

- **CHICKEN MARINADE.** Blend ¼ cup sage leaves with 4 cloves garlic, ⅔ cup oil, juice and zest of 1 lemon. Marinate for up to 4 hours. Or tuck a few sprigs of sage in the cavity or under the skin before roasting.
- **FRY.** Pan-fry sage leaves until crisp and crumble over pumpkin, pork or chicken.
- **PASTA.** For a fast sauce, melt 2–3 tablespoons butter in a pan, add 10 leaves sage and simmer until the butter changes colour and leaves are crisp. Add to cooked ravioli and sprinkle with parmesan.

- **PUMPKIN.** Sage and pumpkin are a match made in heaven. Add to mashed pumpkin or make a dip. Add 2 finely chopped tablespoons to 1 cup mashed pumpkin, 220 g tub cream cheese and couple of tablespoons of grated cheddar.
- **QUICK SAGE AND ONION RELISH.** Serve warm or cold with game, poultry and fish. Sauté 3 onions with 2 tablespoons sage in a little oil, cooking onions slowly until soft but not browned. Add 2 tablespoons balsamic vinegar, ⅓ cup chicken stock and 1 tablespoon honey and cook until the liquid is reduced by half. Keeps in the fridge for a week or two. Makes about ¾ of a cup.
- **RABBIT.** Sage is a perfect foil for the robust flavour of game meats. Brown 4–6 meat pieces, about 1½ kg in total, until coloured then add a finely chopped onion, a couple of cloves of garlic, 2–3 slices chopped bacon and ½ cup chopped sage. Stir for a few minutes and then add 1 cup each white wine and chicken stock. Slow cook, adding more liquid if needed. Add 2 tablespoons red wine vinegar near end of cooking.
- **SAUSAGES AND BEANS.** Brown 5 sausages, set aside. Sauté 1 chopped onion in a little oil, add 2–3 crushed cloves garlic and 1 tablespoon chopped sage. Cook a few minutes. Stir in 2 x 400 g cans cannellini or borlotti beans, 400 g can tomatoes, 1 cup white wine and ½ teaspoon fennel seeds. Bring to a boil; return sausages to pan. Simmer, uncovered, 20 minutes or until sausage is cooked through.
- **STUFFING.** Sage and onion is the traditional stuffing for turkey and duck but it works just as well with other meats. Sauté 4 chopped onions in butter. Combine with ¼ cup chopped sage, 1¼ cups breadcrumbs and 1 lightly beaten egg. This is enough for a medium turkey or a large chicken. Or pack into a small roasting tin to cook separately. It'll take about 30 minutes.
- **VEAL AND CHICKEN.** A great dish that uses sage in the meat and the sauce. Top each thinly sliced veal or chicken fillet with a whole sage leaf, wrap in prosciutto and pan-fry until golden and cooked through. Remove. Add 4 more finely chopped sage leaves to the frypan and cook for 30 seconds. Add ⅓ cup each white wine and chicken stock and reduce by half. Add 1 teaspoon butter and pour over veal or chicken. Serve with beans, potatoes or pasta.

HERB PARTNERS

Sage works well with basil, marjoram, oregano, rosemary, savory and thyme.

Tarragon

Buying

There are two types of tarragon sold in Australia. **French tarragon** is the herb referred to in recipes. It has long slender smooth leaves. **Russian tarragon** is often passed off as the real thing but it has less flavour than its French relation. It has small yellow flowers and slightly serrated, coarser leaves.

Season: Summer only. (Russian tarragon is available during winter.)

HERB PARTNERS

Along with parsley, chives, and chervil, tarragon forms *herbes fines*, the basis of Mediterranean cuisine. Also goes well with dill and marjoram.

Storing

Whole: Wrap in damp paper towel in sealed plastic bag, plastic wrap or airtight container in the fridge. Don't let the leaves get too wet, they go black and lose their flavour. Tarragon keeps for up to five days.

Freezing: Good without affecting flavour.

Using

Best added in the last 30 minutes of cooking.

Using Up

- **ASPARAGUS.** Sprinkle 1 chopped teaspoon tarragon and 1 teaspoon lemon zest over every serving. Also sensational scattered into asparagus soup.
- **BREAD AND BUTTER PICKLES.** Try on hotdogs and hamburgers as well as bread and butter. Cover slices of 2 large cucumbers (or zucchini) and 2 sliced onions with ¼ cup salt and leave for few hours to draw out the liquid. Drain and rinse. Add 1½ cups white or cider vinegar, 1½ cups sugar, 2 tablespoons mustard seeds and 2 tablespoons

chopped tarragon. Cook 2 minutes or until the sugar has dissolved. Pour hot into jars, making sure the liquid covers the cucumbers. Refrigerate. Lasts at least a week.

- **CARROTS.** Sprinkle 1 chopped teaspoon tarragon per serving over honeyed buttered carrots.

- **CHEAT'S FRENCH CHICKEN SALAD.** Add 2 tablespoons tarragon to 1 cup mayonnaise/yoghurt/sour cream and 1–2 tablespoons of what's handy in the pantry, like capers, dill pickles, sweet gherkins, onions, mustard, lemon zest or parsley. Add cooked chicken, celery and spring onions.

- **FRENCH CHICKEN.** Make your own stock and a fragrant cold chicken dish at the same time. Cover an entire chicken with cold water. Add 2–3 sprigs tarragon and roughly chopped stock vegetables i.e. a carrot, a celery stick and an onion (with skin) to the water. Simmer for about an hour. Cool and remove the meat. Strain the stock before reusing.

- **MUSHROOM SALAD.** Dress about 500 grams raw mushrooms with 2 tablespoons tarragon, 1 tablespoon grainy mustard, 2 crushed cloves garlic, ¼ cup balsamic vinegar and ½ cup oil. Refrigerate for ½ hour to let the mushrooms absorb the flavours.

- **PEAS AND LETTUCE.** Sauté 1 chopped onion in a little oil until soft. Add 1 chopped tablespoon tarragon, roughly chopped iceberg lettuce and 2 cups peas. Just cover with water and simmer until the peas are cooked. Serve with chicken or fish.

- **TARTARE SAUCE.** The real stuff has tarragon and it's worth trying even if you're not up to making the mayonnaise. So, to 1 cup of the bought stuff, add 1 heaped finely chopped tablespoon each tarragon, capers and dill pickles as well as the zest of 1 lemon. Keeps in the fridge for up to a week.

- **TUNA AND PASTA SALAD.** Toss together 185 g can tuna and 2 cups cooked pasta. Dress with 1 tablespoon chopped tarragon, 1 tablespoon lemon zest, 1 tablespoon lemon juice, 2 tablespoons white wine vinegar, 1 tablespoon Dijon mustard, 1 small crushed clove garlic and ½ cup olive oil.

- **TUSCAN BREAD SAUCE.** Soak 2–3 slices bread in ¼ cup red wine vinegar. Blend with 2 cloves garlic, ¼ cup tarragon and ½ cup oil until smooth. Keeps in the fridge for a week or so and is lovely with beef, lamb or even a spread for crusty bread.

Thyme

Buying

As well as common thyme, you'll find lemon thyme in Australian supermarkets. It performs pretty much the same in dishes and it really depends on whether or not you want the strong lemon flavour.

WINE WINNER

When you cook with wine, consider thyme (and not just cos it rhymes!) Add a tablespoon to wine-based sauces, marinades and soups whilst cooking.

Storing

Bunch: Wrap in damp paper towel in sealed plastic bag, plastic wrap or airtight container in the fridge. Thyme keeps for up to five days.

Freezing: Good, freeze on the stalk and snip off what you need.

Using

Best added in the last 30 minutes of cooking.

Using Up

- **BEEF STEW.** Thyme is great in slow-cooked dishes. Brown 1 kilogram stewing beef and set aside. Sauté 1 chopped onion in a little oil and add 3 each chopped carrots and celery sticks. Cook 3–5 minutes. Return beef to the pan and add 2½ cups red wine, as many as 8 sprigs thyme, a couple of bay leaves and a tin of tomatoes. Cover and simmer, until beef is tender, about 2 hours. Remove thyme sprigs before serving.
- **BROCCOLI, CHORIZO AND ROASTED RED CAPSICUM RISOTTO.** Fry 2 finely sliced chorizo sausages with 2 tablespoons thyme. Add 1 chopped onion and 2 crushed cloves garlic and sauté in a little oil. Stir in 1 cup risotto rice to coat grains. Gradually add 3–4 cups hot chicken

stock, 1 head broccoli cut into florets, boiling gently and stirring occasionally. Cook until almost all the liquid has been absorbed. Add 2 roasted sliced capsicums. Heat through. Stir in ½ cup parmesan and ¼ cup parsley and serve.

- **BRUSSEL SPROUTS/GREEN BEANS.** Fry 1 kilogram sprouts and/or green beans in 1 tablespoon thyme and 2 slices chopped bacon.

- **LEMON FISH MARINADE.** Marinate fish fillets for up to an hour in lemon juice, lemon zest and thyme. Or see our marinade on p. 150 and replace the Dijon mustard with 1–2 tablespoons thyme leaves. Grill, barbecue or shallow fry until the fish flakes with a fork and serve with wedges of lemon.

- **MEAT MARINADE.** Add three tablespoons to 2 crushed garlic cloves and ¼ cup oil and ¾ cup red wine. Rub into beef, lamb or pork. Leave for up to 4 hours. Or for rabbit and game, up to 8 hours.

- **MINCE.** Add 1 tablespoon thyme to meat loaf, meatballs and bolognaise sauce.

- **PASTA WITH THYME AND FETTA.** Sauté 2 cloves garlic in a little oil, add 1–2 tablespoons thyme leaves and remove from the heat. Add 1 punnet halved cherry tomatoes, 1 cup kalamata olives, 150 grams cubed fetta and enough cooked pasta for 4 people. Add extra oil as needed. Toss and serve.

- **ROASTED THYME BEETROOT SALAD.** Roast 2 beetroot in oil and about 4–5 sprigs thyme. Discard thyme, chop beetroot into bite-sized pieces, add ¼ cup chopped walnuts, 75 grams crumbled goat's cheese and rocket or baby spinach leaves. Dress with 2 tablespoons each oil and lemon juice, and a further teaspoon of thyme leaves.

- **SOUPS.** Place 1 teaspoon thyme leaves in every bowl before serving seafood chowder, chicken and French onion soups.

- **TOMATO JUICE OR BLOODY MARY.** Add a sprig to the jug and chill for a subtle earthy flavour.

- **TURKEY THYME.** Combine 1 tablespoon each chopped parsley, thyme and orange zest with 100 grams butter. Stuff under the skin of the turkey. Fill the cavity with remaining orange, 3–4 sprigs thyme and a head of garlic.

HANDY HINT

Lemon thyme's leaves are softer, so it's easier to use in dishes, like omelettes, where it won't be cooked for long.

HERB PARTNERS

Along with parsley, bay leaves, rosemary and marjoram, thyme forms bouquet garni, the starting point for many stocks, stews and soups.

Have a go

Sabzi Polo

An Iranian dish, where herbs are treated more like green leafy vegetables. The perfect solution to a bumper herb crop. You can leave out the dill and fenugreek if you wish.

Ingredients

1 onion, chopped
750 grams chopped lamb
2 cups rice
1 bunch chives, roughly chopped
1 bunch parsley, roughly chopped
1 bunch dill, roughly chopped
1 bunch coriander, roughly chopped
1 bunch fenugreek, roughly chopped
Pinch saffron

Method

Sauté onion in a little oil. Add meat and brown and seal. Add 1 cup water and cook until the meat is quite tender.

Drain the liquid from the meat (making it up to 3 cups) and cook the rice in it.

Add chopped herbs to the rice and simmer until the liquid is almost absorbed. Place a tea towel over lid and reduce to the lowest heat to let rice steam for about 1 hour

Crush the saffron in a little hot water.

Serve rice with lamb on top and a few stands of saffron.

Lemon

No more excuses for finding a wizened half-lemon in your fridge

You've cut off a slice, grated the peel, or maybe squeezed a bit on your fish. Now what do you do with the bits left over? With our ideas you'll never have to face a wizened half-squeezed lemon at the back of the fridge again. And we've got that bumper crop from the backyard tree covered too.

> **In a few years, all lemons will be seedless. Like seedless grapes and watermelon, it's what the consumer is demanding.** **Kevin P, lemon farmer**

Buying

As well as the sniff test for a decent lemony smell, one of the best indicators is weight. If it's firm and heavy for its size, it's likely to be juicy; if it feels soft, it could be dry.

Thin-skinned lemons are better for juice, thick-skinned for grating (wash thoroughly in warm water to remove any wax). But you can't tell a lemon by its cover: the colour of the peel, whether it's orange, yellow-orange or greenish-yellow, is not an accurate guide to sweetness.

Check the stem as this is where decay usually starts.

Season: Available all year round, but best in the winter months.

WASTE WARRIOR TIP

Got some squeezed lemon halves? Slice them, wrap and freeze – and they'll be ready when you are to pep up your gin and tonic. The more untidy slices are ideal for the water jug, if that's your tipple.

Storing

Whole: Best kept at room temperature, where they last about a week. Lemons will last at least a month in the fridge, though the taste might suffer.

Cut: In fridge, in an airtight container. If you just want a slice or two, save the lemon end and stick it back on. The lemon will last longer.

Peel: In an airtight container in the fridge, though it's better to grate as you need it. However, we were intrigued with the tip to store grated lemon in vodka. Apparently it keeps indefinitely and will not spoil.

Freezing: In an airtight container, whole, halved or sliced.

Using

How much

1 average lemon = 1 tablespoon grated rind
= 3 tablespoons juice
= ¾ cup puree
1 average lime = 2 teaspoons grated rind
= 2 tablespoons juice
= 3 tablespoons puree

Limes may be used in place of lemons, though the flavour is more intense.

You may be able to revive lemons past their prime by popping them in hot water for 30 minutes before using.

If the recipe calls for both zest and juice, it's easier to grate first, then squeeze.

WASTE WARRIOR TIP

Freeze juice in ice-cube trays (squeeze gently without crushing pips or cutting into the pith or you'll make the juice bitter) and then transfer into freezer bags. Measure the size of your ice-cube tray compartments to make it easy to follow recipes.

Especially handy for bumper crops or if you have denuded your lemons for the peel.

Fast preserved lemon

You have a recipe that needs preserved lemon? Quick fix is to boil a whole lemon in very salty water for 30 minutes.

Using Up

Juice – A Squirt or More

A drop in time

Fruit salad. A few drops of lemon juice improves the taste of other fruits and stops apples and bananas from discolouring.

Rice. To make it fluffier, add a few drops to rice while cooking.

Vegetables. To keep the colours bright, squeeze/drizzle lemon on vegetables while steaming.

- **CHIMOLE.** This Latin salsa is at home as a dip or side dish with steaks, fish or chicken. Combine juice 1–2 lemons with 4–5 roughly chopped tomatoes, ¼ finely diced red onion and ½–1 bunch chopped coriander. Keep in fridge, mixing it every now and then, and add a decent pinch of salt shortly before serving (this stops it getting soggy).
- **GREEK LEMON SOUP.** Boil 5 cups chicken stock. Add 2 tablespoons rice and cook about 15 minutes. Just before serving, beat 2 eggs until they are light and frothy, then slowly beat in juice 1 lemon. Gradually stir egg mixture into 1 cup hot soup. Pour into rest of the soup, beating well. Heat, but don't boil, or the soup will curdle. Serve immediately.

WASTE WARRIOR TIP

Rather than cutting open a whole lemon/lime for just a little juice, you can make a hole with a skewer or toothpick and squeeze out the amount of juice you need. Wrap the fruit and it'll stay fresh in the fridge for 1–2 weeks.

Spare Halves, Wedges, and Slices

- **CHICKEN STUFFING.** Cut up squeezed lemon halves or wedges and put inside the cavity of a whole chicken before roasting, along with a couple of rosemary sprigs, a bulb of garlic and a big knob of butter.
- **FISH.** Place thinly sliced lemons, peel and all, underneath and around fish before baking. The slices will be so soft you can eat them.
- **SANGRIA.** Add to sangria or white wine spritzers.

I'll drink to that

Coffee. Add grated peel to coffee grounds for a fresh flavour.

Teapot. Add dried peel to your brew.

- **BAKING.** Zest up your biscuits, cakes, pies and tarts.
- **BREAKFAST CEREAL.** Sprinkle on hot or cold cereals for extra flavour.
- **BUTTER.** Whip into butter for toast or cooking. Add some mustard for that extra touch.
- **CARBONATED DRINKS.** Add to commercial lemonade to make it taste more like homemade, as well as to cola drinks for a refreshing tartness.
- **FROSTING.** Add flavour to icing and frosting.
- **GLAZE.** Add to a mix of honey and soy sauce to brush on chicken.

PIP TIP

Wrap a small piece of cheesecloth around the cut end of a lemon before you squeeze into your drink or over your fish. You won't have to search for pips later.

Substitutions

Sour cream substitute. Add 2 teaspoons lemon juice to 1 cup cream and leave for 20 minutes.

Salt substitute. Try the tartness of lemon wedges instead.

- **GREMOLATA.** Basic recipe is 3 tablespoons parsley, 1 crushed clove garlic and 1 teaspoon grated peel. Some add a little olive oil. Traditionally spooned over osso bucco. Equally good with steamed vegies.
- **MUFFINS.** Put a teaspoon in blueberry or poppyseed muffin mix.
- **SALADS.** Sprinkle on for a lemony flourish.

CITRUS SUGAR

Store grated rind in a jar of sugar to sprinkle over cereal, porridge and pancakes.

Juicy hints

What's the best way to get the most juice from your lemons?

- Take the lemon out of the fridge at least 30 minutes before you want to use it. Press and roll on the kitchen table to soften, making it easier to squeeze.
- Prick the skin with a fork and zap in the microwave for 10 seconds.
- Put in hot water for 15 minutes to get nearly twice as much juice.

These tips also work for oranges.

- **CEVICHE.** Popular in Central and South America. In Panama, it's eaten with crackers, in Mexico on toasted tortillas, in Peru they like it with corn on the cob, and Ecuador with potato chips. Combine finely sliced onion, finely chopped chilli or dash of Tabasco, a handful of chopped coriander and maybe a crushed clove of garlic. Add your choice of raw fresh seafood cut into bite-sized pieces. Cover the lot with lemon juice (about 1 cup for 500 grams fish) and leave in the fridge for 2 hours or more, stirring now and then. Ready when fish turns from transparent to opaque. Serve as an entrée in lettuce leaves or avocado shells. **If you have it:** Add tiny cubes of tomato, cucumber or avocado just before serving. Any citrus juice will do the same marinating job. For salt and sugar cured fish see Gravlax p. 129.
- **FISH MARINADE.** Combine ⅔ cup lemon juice, 2 teaspoons grated lemon, 1 crushed clove garlic, 3 tablespoons Dijon mustard, a touch of sugar and maybe some paprika. Add about ⅓ cup water. Pour over fish for up to an hour before cooking. Good with chicken too.
- **LEMONADE.** Heat ¾ cup sugar with 1 cup water in a saucepan and stir until sugar dissolves. Cool. Add 1–1½ cups

lemon juice to taste. Mix with 3 cups soda water and serve with lemon slices and sprigs of mint.

- **PORK MARINADE.** Combine juice and grated peel 3 lemons, 1 tablespoon each honey, olive oil and chopped mint, and 1 teaspoon each ground coriander, paprika and ground cumin.
- **SYLLABUB.** Doesn't sound like it, but it's an Olde English recipe. Combine ¼ cup caster sugar, 2 teaspoons finely grated lemon rind and 2 tablespoons lemon juice and heat gently until sugar dissolves. Let the mixture cool a little then add ½ cup sweet white wine. Whip about 1¼ cups thickened cream to soft peaks and fold into the mixture. Serve with strawberries.
- **TUNA.** Chop up 4–6 lemons – removing all the pips, pith and membranes. Add a 400 g can tuna (or salmon) and mix in ¼ cup chopped flat leaf parsley with sour cream or mayonnaise to bind it all together. **If you have it:** Add some pitted black olives and dill. Use large lemon shells as serving dishes.

FANCY TOUCH

Citrus peel makes an impressive garnish.

Curls. Wrap long strips of lemon, lime or grapefruit peel around a chopstick for at least 30 minutes and cut to the length you want.

Ribbons. Tie your asparagus or beans with a citrus ribbon. Use a sharp paring knife to get nice, even strips.

A Little Effort

- **CURD.** Serve on toast or as a topping for yoghurt or ice-cream. Combine ⅓ cup butter, grated rind and juice 2 large lemons, 1 cup caster sugar and 3 eggs in the top of a double saucepan and stir constantly with a wooden spoon until the mixture thickens. Pour into jars. Keeps in fridge for up to a month. Makes about 3 cups.
- **LEMON CHUTNEY.** Serve with roast or cold chicken and cheeses. Combine 6 large lemons cut into thin rounds (discarding the pips) and 250 g finely chopped onions. Sprinkle mixture with 1½ tablespoons salt, leave in fridge for 24 hours. Drain. Simmer mixture, just covered in water, over a low heat until the lemon peel is soft but not broken. Add 1¾ cups cider vinegar, 1 cup sugar, ½ cup sultanas and 1½ tablespoons white mustard seeds and 1 teaspoon ground ginger. Bring to the boil. Reduce heat and simmer for 1 hour stirring frequently. Pour into hot jars. Store for 1 month before using. Makes 2–3 cups.

Meat

Make a starter from meaty morsels – plus ideas to ham it up

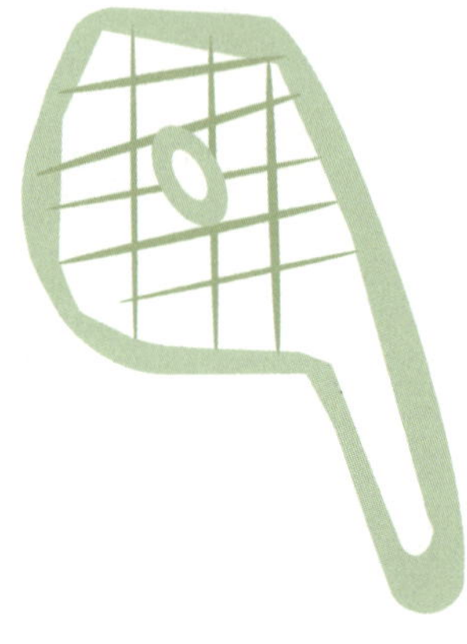

The problem with meat is that once you've cooked it, it doesn't freeze well unless it has a sauce. If throwing out leftover roast makes you feel especially guilty then this is the chapter for you. In fact, these tips may tempt you to deliberately cook too much next time.

> **Roasted toasted sandwiches are my favourite after a dinner party. Add fetta and some oregano to roast lamb, or tzatziki to make a yiros sandwich. Roast beef is great with horseradish and some rocket. Pork goes with apple sauce. You get the drift ... Bunty P**

Buying

Raw Meat

Buy last, take straight home, and store immediately in the fridge or freezer. If you can, use an insulated bag or wrap your meat in layers of paper to keep it as cool as possible until you get it home.

Fresh: Buy only from a refrigerated display.

Frozen: Make sure it's been stored below the 'load line' – usually about five centimetres below the rim of the cabinet. Avoid packs with ice crystals inside or clumps of ice between them as this can mean they've been badly stored or re-frozen.

Storing

Raw: If you're using the meat the same day you buy it, just pop in the fridge in its original wrapping.

To store longer, take it out of any plastic wrap as it makes the meat sweat. Cover the meat with foil or loose plastic wrap so that air can circulate. Put it in the coldest part of the fridge – usually the bottom shelf. Make sure the juices don't drip onto other food.

Never store raw and cooked meats together or raw meat with other foods, especially salads.

Food	Fridge	Freezer
Sausages	2 days	1–2 months
Mince (beef and lamb) Beef and lamb strips Diced meat Thin steaks (minute)	2 days	2–3 months
Steaks	2–3 days	3–4 months
Roasts (boned and rolled)	2–3 days	4–6 months
Roasts (bone in)	3–4 days	4–6 months
Corned beef (fresh)	1 week	4–6 months
Vacuum packed meat (unopened)	Up to 8 weeks in the coldest part of the fridge (below 4 °C)	4–6 months
Cooked meals	3–4 days	2–3 months

Cooked: Cool down as quickly as possible: shallow containers work faster than deep ones. Also, metal containers are good because they lose heat faster than thick plastic ones. Put meat in the fridge uncovered until cooled, then cover the container or wrap meat in plastic wrap.

Roasts left on the bone stay moist and firm.

Freezing

Raw: Use good quality freezer bags, making sure all the air has been squeezed out.

Cooked: Stews, casseroles and mince dishes freeze very well. Make sure the meat is covered with liquid – adding a little water if necessary – or it will dry out. This is why cooked steaks and meat loaf don't freeze well.

One way to make sure the packages are airtight is to use containers lined with plastic bags.

Thawing

Raw: Best to thaw in the bottom of the fridge so it doesn't drip onto other food. A rule of thumb is 10 hours for every 500 g of meat. Alternatively, thaw it in cold water (in airtight packaging), changing the water every 30 minutes. Once defrosted, meat keeps in the fridge for one day, two at the most, before cooking.

It's not a good idea to thaw at room temperature. If you have no choice, the best advice is to thaw, cook and eat. Don't put it back in the fridge. It's the same with thawing in the microwave. Make sure you unwrap meat for microwave thawing or the liquid will boil and the meat will turn grey. Styrofoam trays are not microwave safe.

Mince

Buying: What grade of mince to buy? The leanest is best for hamburgers and bolognaise sauce while mince with a little more fat is good for meatballs, kofta and meat loaf.

Storing: Best to use as soon as possible and well within the use-by date. Loose mince from the butcher is best used within one or two days.

If you notice raw mince is brown beneath the surface, don't panic. It's just that the top layer has been exposed to air, making it red. But if it's grey-brown right through that could mean it's spoiled. Throw it out.

Freezing: Flatten out that ball of mince first. It takes up less space and will freeze and thaw more evenly. Freeze for up to three months.

Thawing: Best in the fridge. If using a microwave, remove outer portions as it softens.

Using: To kill any possible bacteria, thoroughly cook until there are no pink bits. Reheat to steaming for the same reason. Meals keep in fridge for three or four days, in freezer for up to three months.

Using

How much

180 grams cooked meat = 1 cup

It may be safe to cook raw meat before it's completely thawed, but you'll have to cook for longer and probably chew on it longer. Is it really worth it?

One exception: you can pop frozen corned beef straight into boiling water. Just add a few more minutes to allow for the thawing time in the hot water.

Be light-handed when basting with marinades during cooking: if you just pour it on, it makes the meat stew and causes flare-ups.

HANDY (HEALTHY) HINT

If you're planning on using the marinade after you've been soaking raw meat or poultry, boil it first. This will kill any harmful bacteria.

Tender tips for steaks

They get tough if you turn too often or use too low a heat.

Don't use salt before cooking as it draws out the juices and will make the meat tough.

Test meat by pressing with blunt tongs to see the colour of the juices. If you cut with a knife to test, the juices will escape and the meat will be dry.

Tender tips for roasts

Let the meat 'rest' before carving to let the juices absorb through the meat. Rest a roast for 10 to 20 minutes, steaks or chops for 2 to 3 minutes.

Cover meat loosely with foil to keep hot before serving – not tightly as the meat will sweat.

Cut against the grain. Cutting along the grain will make the meat chewy.

Using Up

Any Cooked Meat

- **BURRITOS.** Chop leftover **roast** or **grilled** meat finely. Mix in some meat stock or gravy flavoured with cumin and oregano. Add a finely chopped chilli. Roll up in flour tortillas.

- **MEATBALLS.** Blend or chop finely the remains of the **roast**. Add finely chopped onion, 1 egg and seasoning. Mould into balls. Fry until golden and simmer in tomato sauce until heated through. **If you have it:** Add chopped rosemary and oregano to lamb. Or push a cube of cheese in the centre of each meatball.

- **PASTIES.** Finely chop or shred remains of the **roast**. Sauté onion in a little oil, then add finely diced cooked potato, carrot, swede or turnip with herbs and seasoning. Put spoonfuls of mixture in the middle of shortcrust or puff pastry rounds. Brush edges with egg and milk, fold over and seal tightly. Make a slit in the top, brush all over with egg or milk and bake in moderate oven until golden.

The 2–4 hour rule

Don't eat cooked meat that's been left out the fridge for more than four hours in total.

If it's been at room temperature for less than 2 hours, you can stick it in the fridge and bring it out later. If it's been at room temperature for more than 2 hours, it's too late to put in the fridge. Eat it before the 4 hours are up. (Also applies for cooked rice and vegetables, prepared salads, milk and processed foods containing eggs.)

- **SALADS.** Ideal for slightly underdone **roast** meat. Try slicing thinly and laying on a bed of lettuce, topping with bean sprouts and mango or orange slices. Pour over a Thai dressing of ¼ cup fresh lime juice, ¾ cup finely chopped coriander, a few mint leaves, ½ tablespoon olive oil, 1 tablespoon fish sauce, 2 teaspoons brown sugar, 1 teaspoon finely grated fresh ginger and 1 tablespoon sweet chilli sauce.

- **SHEPHERD'S PIE.** Under cover of mashed potato, you can do all sorts of wonderful things with the remains of any meat dish. The basic recipe for the meat base is to sauté a couple of chopped onions in a little oil until soft, mix in 2 cups finely chopped or minced cooked lamb, and moisten with ½ cup stock and Worchestershire sauce. (Apparently it's called cottage pie if you use beef.) Cover with mashed potato. Bake in a hot oven for 30 minutes. **If you have it:** Add garlic, tomatoes, parsley and red wine. Or sprinkle top with grated cheese.

- **SOUPS.** Puree beef or lamb **stew** to make a thick soup, adding extra stock or water if necessary. Or thinly slice remains of **roasts** or **steak** and add to Asian-style broth made with vegetable stock, some soy sauce, chilli, juice ½ lime and chopped coriander and fresh mint.

- **SPAGHETTI SAUCE.** Make a mean, meaty sauce with leftover **meat loaf**, **hamburgers** or **patties**. Just mince or chop finely and add to your favourite tomato sauce and pour over pasta. Or make lasagne.

Beef

- **MIROTON.** A favourite French meal from leftover meat. Good for **boiled**, **roast** and **grilled** beef. Sauté 2 chopped onions in 2 tablespoons butter until soft and transparent. Add 1 crushed clove garlic. Mix in ¼ cup plain flour, stirring constantly until lightly browned and the mixture leaves the side of the pot. Add 1 tablespoon red wine vinegar and 1 cup stock, stirring until sauce thickens. You may need to add up to another cup of stock. Add 2 tablespoons tomato paste and 1 teaspoon French mustard. Bring to the boil then simmer for 20 minutes. Slice beef wafer-thin and arrange on the bottom of casserole. Pour over sauce, sprinkle over breadcrumbs mixed with parsley and a little melted butter and brown in hot oven. Serve with a green salad.

- **PYTT I PANNA.** Here is Sweden's version of meat and potato hash. The trick is to dice everything finely. Dice 4 peeled potatoes, 1–2 cups cooked beef, 4 slices bacon and 2 onions. Fry potatoes for about 15 minutes until crisp. Remove and keep warm. Fry onions, meat and bacon for about 10 minutes until cooked. Add potatoes and cook a further 5–10 minutes. Mix in 1 tablespoon chopped parsley. **If you have it:** The traditional method is to make a hole in the centre of each serve and crack in a raw egg, which each person then mixes through with a few drops of Worchestershire sauce and Tabasco. Or you could poach or fry the eggs beforehand.
- **STROGANOFF.** Especially good with slices from the pink centre of a **roast**. Sauté 1 large sliced onion in butter for a couple of minutes. Add 1 crushed clove garlic, 1 tablespoon paprika and 1 cup sliced mushrooms and cook until onion and mushrooms are soft. Stir in 2 tablespoons tomato puree and ½ cup sour cream and simmer gently for 5 minutes. Add finely sliced meat and heat through. Serve with boiled rice or noodles.

Lamb

- **KORMA.** Sauté 1 chopped onion in a little oil for 2 minutes. Add 2 crushed cloves garlic, a 5-centimetre knob grated ginger, 1 tablespoon garam masala, 1 teaspoon turmeric and 2 tablespoons ground almonds and cook for a couple more minutes. Add chopped vegetables such as mushrooms, peas, carrots, cauliflower and capsicum and 1 cup stock. Stir in 400 mL can coconut milk, bring to the boil and then simmer for 5–10 minutes until the vegetables are tender. Stir in chopped lamb (**roast** or leftover **chops**) at the end. Serve with natural yoghurt and chutney.
- **KOFTA BALLS.** Finely chop or mince 1 cup or so of leftover lamb. Add 1 egg, 2 tablespoons each mint and coriander or flat leaf parsley, 1 teaspoon ground coriander and a hefty pinch of cumin. Add ¼ cup soft breadcrumbs or enough to help bind the mixture. Makes 8 kofta balls. Chill in fridge for ½ hour before frying in hot oil for 2–3 minutes on each side. Serve with tzatziki and a tomato salad.

Meat stock

The bones from a roast make a great stock. (Throw them in the freezer to make when you have more time.)

Here are the basic steps:

1. Baste bones with oil and salt. Roast in a hot oven for 30–40 minutes until quite brown to give stronger flavour and richer colour.

2. Cover with cold water and add chopped vegetables and herbs. Bring slowly to the boil, remove scum from the surface, reduce heat and simmer for about 4 hours. Usual vegetables include onions, carrots, leeks, celery. Herbs and seasonings include bay leaf, parsley, thyme and peppercorns.

3. Continually check water level and top up with hot water to keep ingredients covered.

4. Cool and strain, discarding bones and vegetables. Remove fat by laying a piece of paper towel over the surface and soaking it up. (Then remove the paper, of course.)

If the stock's not going to be used immediately, leave the fat to settle on the surface. When you want to use it, it's easy to lift off.

Keeps in fridge 4–5 days.

Freeze in recipe portions. Keeps up to 3 months.

- **MOUSSAKA.** Sauté 2 thinly sliced eggplants in a little oil until soft. Remove. Sauté 3 sliced onions in little oil. Add 2 cups minced or finely chopped cooked lamb, 1 tablespoon rosemary, ½ cup stock, good splash of red wine and 2 tablespoons tomato puree. Line dish with half the eggplant slices, top with meat mixture and finish with another layer of eggplant. Bake in moderate oven 30 minutes. Melt 50 grams butter, stir in 2 tablespoons plain flour and cook for a few minutes before whisking in 1½ cups milk. Stir over medium heat until it boils. Whisk in 1 egg. Pour over the meat, sprinkle with ½ cup grated cheese and return to oven for another 20 minutes until there's a golden crust. **If you have it:** Add a layer of sliced ripe tomatoes after the meat mixture.

- **SCOTCH BROTH.** Add 2 onions, 2 carrots, 1 turnip or swede and 1 leek, all finely chopped, and 1 sprig thyme to 8 cups stock. (Best with stock made from lamb shanks.) Soak ½ cup pearl barley in plenty of water for 1 hour before draining and adding to vegetable mixture. Bring to the boil and simmer for about 1 hour until barley and vegetables are cooked. Add lamb from the **shanks** along with ½ cup parsley and serve.

Ham it up

A Christmas ham is compulsory for many families, even those who hardly touch bacon or pork the rest of the year. And those leftovers appear to be an institution as well, taking up precious space in a fridge otherwise reserved for cold beers.

- **CANNELLONI.** Sauté 1 finely chopped onion, 2 crushed cloves garlic and 1 chopped green capsicum in a little butter or oil. Add 1–2 cups cubed ham. Leave to cool. Stir in ⅓ cup parmesan cheese. Make 1 cup cheese sauce. The white mould one (see p. 88) works well with any cheese. Mix ¼ of sauce with ham mixture and stuff into cannelloni shells. Pour half of the remaining sauce in a greased baking dish. Put shells on sauce and top with rest of sauce. Sprinkle with ½ cup parmesan cheese, and bake in moderate oven for 30–35 minutes.

SAFETY FIRST

You don't have to wait until food is cold to put it in the fridge. Just wait until it's stopped steaming. Most fridges will cope if the food is around 45 °C.

- **FRITTERS.** Make a smooth batter with 1 cup self-raising flour, 2 eggs and ⅓ cup milk. Add 1 cup chopped ham, 420 g can corn kernels (rinsed and drained), 1 finely chopped red capsicum, 1 small finely chopped red onion and 4 tablespoons chopped chives. Fry 1 heaped tablespoon batter for each fritter for 2–3 minutes each side until golden. Makes 12.
- **PASTA.** Combine semidried tomatoes, chopped ham, olives and basil and gently toss through the pasta until well combined.
- **PIZZA.** Add to your pizza topping – with or without pineapple!
- **POTATO CAKES.** Boil 5 medium potatoes and roughly mash. Add 1 cup chopped ham, 1 egg, 4 chopped spring onions, ⅓ cup dried breadcrumbs, ¼ cup flat leaf parsley, salt and pepper. Shape into patties and fry in oil for 5 minutes each side until golden.

- **POTTED HAM.** Coarsely mince or chop 2 cups ham and add to ¼ cup melted butter. Season with a pinch each of marjoram and mace. Cook gently for 3 minutes. Pack meat into small pots or terrine. Melt 1 tablespoon butter until foaming. Strain through muslin over the meat. Leave to cool. Serve with toast.
- **RISOTTO.** Got some sage left over from the turkey stuffing? This is the dish for you. Sauté 1 chopped onion in a little oil, add 2 crushed cloves garlic and 1 cup chopped ham. Stir in 2 cups risotto rice to coat grains. Gradually add 4–5 cups hot stock and 1 cup white wine, boiling gently and stirring occasionally. Cook until almost all the liquid has been absorbed. Add 1 cup thawed frozen peas and a dozen finely chopped sage leaves. Heat through. Stir in ½ cup parmesan and serve.

Finally, you can add chopped ham to many of the recipes in the chicken chapter.

Don't be left in the dark about these fungi

They may start out plump but it doesn't take long before you're harbouring a couple of wrinkled specimens or a whole bag of desiccated well intentions. Far from being bad news, this is the starting point for a whole world of flavour.

Dietlicious

Mushies may be the perfect diet food. They're very low in kilojoules and they've been shown to make you feel full. Recent Australian research also suggests they may even reduce your appetite.

Buying

Up to 98 per cent of all the mushrooms sold in Australia are the white *Agaricus* variety. From the cute little ones to the big fleshy mushrooms – they are all *Agaricus*, just picked at different stages of its life. (The other 2 per cent are mainly Swiss browns, shiitake and oyster mushrooms.)

Button mushrooms have flesh closed tightly around the stem. They're the youngest but not necessarily the smallest.

The flavour of the mushroom develops as the cap opens. These are called **cups**.

Flat mushrooms, as their name suggests, have fully opened and flattened caps, exposing dark, velvety gills. They're not field mushrooms, although they look and taste pretty similar.

Season: All year round. Best value in peak season from March to June.

Variety	Use
Buttons	Mild flavour – perfect for salads, or with dips. Readily absorb other flavours so suit pasta and stir-fry.
Cups	More intense flavour, most versatile. Try in soups, sauces and stews
Flats	Most intense flavour – perfect for barbecue, soup, tapenade, sauce and gravy.

Storing

Fresh: Stick them straight in the fridge in the paper bag you bought them in. Best on the shelf above the crisper because the crisper itself can be so humid that the bag falls apart (though the mushrooms will be fine). If the mushrooms are covered in plastic or in a container where they can't breathe, they will sweat and become slimy pretty quickly. Transfer to a paper or cloth bag or maybe a plate lined with paper towel. Some people swear by an earthen or ceramic bowl but the experts haven't been able to detect any difference.

Mushrooms last for three days up to a week.

The younger **button** mushrooms don't necessarily last longer than **cups** or **flats**.

Freezing: Yes, but you do have to cook them just a little first. Either blanch for three or four minutes or sauté in butter and/or oil. (If blanching, you may want to prevent the mushrooms from darkening. Before cooking, soak for five minutes in a solution of one teaspoon of lemon juice for every two cups of water.)

Cooked: Mushroom dishes keep for a couple of days in a sealed container in the fridge and freeze well for months.

HANDY HINT

Don't throw away wrinkled mushrooms. Use in cooked dishes. They're ageing, sure, but their main problem is dehydration and they'll plump up when they come into contact with moisture.

Using

How much

4–5 buttons (approx 4 centimetres in diameter)
= 100 grams
3–4 cups (approx 6 centimetres in diameter)
= 100 grams
½ flat (approx 15 centimetres in diameter)
= 100 grams

To wash or not to wash?

We know some of you don't wash mushrooms but you can. It won't hurt them or reduce their flavour, even if you're eating them raw. (Though they go a little slimy which may be a turn-off.)

Certainly, there's no need to peel, most of the nutrients are in the skin after all. If you're cooking mushrooms, simply brush the dirt away.

Exotic mushroom substitutions

Shiitake	Nameko, cinnamon caps or trumpet royale
Swiss browns or portobello	Sulfur mushrooms, aka chicken-of-the-woods, or matsutake
Oyster	Maitake or fresh chanterelles

Using Up

A Few Wizened Mushrooms

- **BARBECUE.** Especially good for a couple of larger mushies in danger of going to waste. Paint both sides with a combination of ⅓ cup oil and 2 tablespoons Worcestershire sauce. Chargrill for 1 minute on each side. (Cook over a chargrilling plate so you get those brown stripes like it has just come off the barbie.) Use a large mushroom instead of the meat in a hamburger. **If you have it:** Add 1 tablespoon of chopped herbs, parsley, chives or basil to the baste.
- **JACKET POTATO.** Sauté whatever mushrooms you have in little oil with 1 crushed clove garlic and a splash of cream to top a baked potato.
- **PASTA CARBONARA.** This egg and bacon pasta sauce is lovely with mushrooms (see p. 110). Also add to lasagne or any tomato-based sauce.

I always make sure I put them in spaghetti bolognaise and not pissy little slices but big fat wedges. You have got to have the flavour of them in the sauce.

Ben P

- **MINCE.** Add chopped mushrooms to any minced meat dish, including meat loaf and meatballs.
- **QUICHE/FRITTATA/OMELETTE/PIE.** Chop and add to any flavour combination. Good with zucchini slice and quiche Lorraine as well as chicken and fish pies.
- **ROASTED MARINATED VEGIES WITH FETTA.** Chop a selection of vegetables that roast well into bite-sized pieces, including mushrooms. Consider pumpkin, capsicum, eggplant, tomatoes, red onion slices and crushed cloves of garlic. Drizzle with oil and roast, shaking the pan once or twice to turn them, for 30 minutes. Toss with 125 grams fetta. Serve warm or at room temperature with barbecue lamb, chicken or chops.
- **STIR-FRY.** Chop and add to any stir-fry.

A Wizened Glut

- **BREAD PUDDING.** Sauté 4 leeks and 500 grams mushrooms in butter with 4 crushed cloves garlic and 1 tablespoon thyme leaves. Add ½ cup white wine and cook until it has evaporated and the mushrooms have browned. Spread 5–6 cups day-old breadcrumbs onto bottom of buttered baking dish. Spoon mushroom mixture on top and pour over six lightly beaten eggs combined with 1 cup milk, ½ cup cream, ½ cup stock and 1 cup grated cheese. Rest for ½ hour in fridge for bread to absorb mushroom mixture. Bake for about 40 minutes in moderate oven or until the top is brown.
- **DEEP FRIED.** To coat 400 grams mushrooms: combine 3 cups breadcrumbs, ⅓ cup chives and 2 teaspoons curry powder (optional). Lightly beat 3 eggs. Dip 1 mushroom at a time into egg mixture, then breadcrumbs, pressing the breadcrumbs to secure. Deep-fry in batches for 2–3 minutes or until golden.

- **HUMMUS.** Mushrooms are lovely stuffed with hummus. This dip combines the two flavours. Sauté 2 crushed cloves garlic in a little oil with 1 tablespoon cumin until soft. Add 400 grams chopped mushrooms and cook 5 minutes or until mushrooms are just tender. Blend 300 g can chickpeas, 2 tablespoons tahini, 2 tablespoons lemon juice and ¼ cup oil until smooth. Stir mushroom and chickpea mixtures together with ½ cup chopped chives. Makes 3 cups. Great with lamb, along with a dollop of yoghurt.

- **INDIAN TOMATO AND MUSHROOMS.** Sauté 1 chopped onion and 1 crushed clove garlic in a little oil. Add chilli to taste and 1 teaspoon each cardamom, black pepper, nutmeg, cumin, ground coriander and turmeric. Cook for 1 minute or until fragrant. Add 600 grams mushrooms and combine for 30 seconds. Add 3 cups tomato sauce (or 400 g can tomatoes and 1 tablespoon tomato paste). Simmer for 20 minutes. Serve with crushed peanuts and flat bread.

- **JAPANESE FISH SAUCE.** Sauté 1 chopped onion in a little oil with 400 grams mushrooms until tender. Add 2 tablespoons each soy sauce and mirin (or substitute sweet sherry) and cook for few minutes. Add ½ cup chicken stock to mushroom mixture. Pour over steamed white fish or tofu and serve in a bowl. **If you have it:** Use dashi (Japanese stock) instead of chicken stock.

- **PRAWN SALAD.** You might not think your mushrooms are good enough for a salad, but soak in salad dressing and they will plump up. Slice 300 grams and pour over a dressing of ¼ cup honey, 2 tablespoons balsamic vinegar and ⅓ cup olive oil. Marinate for 30 minutes. Add 1 diced avocado and 350 grams peeled cooked prawns. **If you have it:** Toss in 6 thinly sliced spring onions, ⅓ cup chives before serving. Add 1 tablespoon grated ginger or grainy mustard in the dressing.

- **SATAY MUSHROOMS.** Combine ¼ cup peanut paste, ½ cup coconut milk, 2 tablespoons soy sauce and 1 tablespoon sugar and heat. Sauté 2 crushed cloves garlic, chilli to taste and 700 grams mushrooms in a little oil until just tender. Add mushrooms to sauce, tossing constantly for 2–3 minutes. Serve with steamed rice.

- **SIMPLE TARTS.** Pre-prepare individual homemade bases or follow instructions on packet. Sauté 500 grams mushrooms and 1 chopped onion in a little oil until they begin to brown. Cook 250 grams frozen spinach or 1 chopped fresh bunch until wilted. Drain well. Spoon a little of each mixture into pastry cases and top with 100 grams crumbled goat's cheese. Bake in moderate oven until cheese is lightly browned, about 15 minutes.

- **SOUP.** Sauté 1 chopped onion, 3 crushed cloves garlic and 600 grams sliced mushrooms in butter. Cook for 10 minutes or until tender. Add 5 cups stock, stirring constantly. Bring to the boil stirring. Reduce heat and simmer 10 minutes, stirring occasionally. Puree and stir in ¼–½ cup cream and ½ cup chopped parsley. **If you have it:** Squeeze lemon juice and/or lemon zest over each bowl.

- **STIR-FRY.** Mushrooms shine in this quick cook method. Think soy sauce, garlic, ginger, honey, Chinese five spice, sesame seeds and hoisin sauce. Or try walnuts and lemon. Stir-fry 2 crushed cloves garlic and 500 grams mushrooms until just tender. Combine 2 teaspoons brown sugar, 1 tablespoon balsamic vinegar and 2 tablespoons lemon. Add to mushrooms and stir-fry 30 seconds or until well coated. Remove from the heat and stir through 1 cup toasted walnuts (a few minutes in a wok, frypan or microwave). Serve with rice.

No-tears tips and how to make onions the centre of attention

Onions are so important to many cultures that some cuisines would all but disappear without them. So, it's a fine line between having a good supply and getting caught with half a bag of sprouting onions that need to be used, pronto. This is where the onion really comes into its own.

> **My father used to chop up the onions for the relish and the like and he used to wear welding goggles. He'd chop up a baby's bathful!** **Lyn S**

Stop crying over sliced onions ...

- The only sure-fire way? Goggles.
- The next best solution? Chilling or cooking the onion before chopping. Although this can still leave you blubbering.
- Less reliable, and somewhat impractical: chopping under running water.
- The only slightly helpful: turning on a fan/opening all the windows.
- The utterly ineffectual: breathing through your mouth only.

The good news is that some onions are less teary than others, even though they look the same. Queensland-grown brown onions are less pungent (and a little softer). It's the soil, apparently. They hit the shops between November and February.

Buying

Onions should be shiny and dry, with a papery outer skin. Choose those that are heavy for their size and solid all over with a tightly closed neck.

Sprouting onions are ageing and starting to dry out – they won't be as tasty as fresher ones.

WASTE WARRIOR POWER

The onion may or may not be able to keep evil spirits at bay, but it does have great power. In fact, the largest onion processor in the US has recently started to use onion juice to make electricity. The Californian-based company wanted to do something with their onion waste because they were losing up to 40 per cent of the onion in peelings. The juice they now extract from the waste is very high in sugars. Bacteria love it, producing methane gas and helping the company cut its power bills and greenhouse gas emissions.

Storing

Whole: In a cool, dry, ventilated place away from bright light. Not in the fridge for extended periods, except in hot humid climates where the best option might be the warmest part, i.e. the fridge door. The one exception is spring onions – keep them in the crisper.

Onions absorb moisture. So, don't keep below the sink, or in plastic bags without holes. If moisture is a problem, try wrapping individually in paper towels.

Onions keep for two weeks to two months, depending on the variety. As a general rule, the sharper the flavour, the longer they keep.

Cut: In an airtight container in the fridge for up to seven days.

Freezing: It's possible but they soften and lose some of their flavour. So, you'll need to add more to your cooking than with fresh to get the same flavour.

Don't bother blanching before freezing, just peel and chop. You can then take them straight from the freezer to the pan or cooking pot. Frozen onions keep up to three months.

Cooked: Caramelised onion keeps well in an airtight container in fridge for several days.

Variety	Best from	Flavour	Storage	Use
Brown	Sept–March	Strongest flavoured	Keeps longest, up to a month	Best for soups and casseroles
White	July–Jan	Milder than brown with slightly sweeter flavour	About 3 weeks	Can be eaten both raw (in salads) or cooked
Red or Spanish Onion	Oct–March	Milder and sweeter than brown or white	2–4 weeks	Best eaten raw in salsas and salads and lovely barbecued or roasted
Spring onion (also called green onion, scallion, green shallots)		The green tops are very mild, the white section is stronger	1 week	Use in salads and dips or as a garnish. The white section is stronger but can still be eaten raw and is well suited to stir-fries

Using

How much

1 medium onion = 1 cup chopped
= 180 grams
3 or 4 onions = 1 cup caramelised

There is nothing wrong with eating sprouted onions: they're just old and they don't taste as strong.

You can use any onion in our Using Up section, except brown onions in crumbed onion rings and pakora – they are too strong.

Using Up

A Few Spare Sprouted (or threatening to)

- **CHARGRILLED SALAD.** Your onion is never too sad to make a salad. Just hack off the bad bits and cut into thick slices, paint with oil and chargrill. (Cook over a chargrilling plate so you get those brown stripes like it has just come off the barbie.) Then all you need for your salad is to add a couple of chopped tomatoes or a sliced orange. **If you have it:** Add a dressing of 1 tablespoon each lime or orange juice, olive oil and chopped coriander/basil/oregano.
- **CHEAT'S ONION CHUTNEY.** Serve over chicken, sausages, hotdogs and hamburgers. Spice up fruit chutneys, like mango, by adding 1 sautéed onion, chilli to taste and 1 tablespoon sugar to each ¼ cup. **If you have it:** Add 1 tablespoon fresh herbs, such as parsley, basil, coriander or tarragon.
- **CREAMED.** Simmer quartered onion in a couple of centimetres chicken stock, covered, for about 30 minutes, until very tender, adding water if it looks like drying out. Uncover and let liquid reduce. Add a generous splash of cream and minced fresh thyme. Simmer but don't boil, for a few minutes.
- **CRUMBED.** Dip finely sliced white or red onion rings into flour, then beaten egg, then seasoned breadcrumbs. Fry in a few centimetres of hot oil, 6 or 8 at a time, for 6–7 minutes, turning once, until a deep golden brown.
- **ROAST.** Peel, quarter and toss in oil. Roast for 40 minutes in a hot oven or until deeply browned. Sprinkle with balsamic vinegar (about 1 tablespoon for 2 onions) and continue to roast until brown and glazed. **If you have it:** Sprinkle fresh or even dried herbs over onion before cooking.

DID YOU KNOW?

Spring onions are just immature onions, picked before the bulb has grown. So, they can be red, white, purple or yellow.

An Overabundance of Old Onions

- **FRENCH ONION SOUP.** Easier than you expect and tastier than you remember. Very French, really. Even though we've added Vegemite. Sauté 8 chopped onions and 2 minced cloves garlic in oil and butter over low heat, until the onions are very soft and brown, but not burnt. Sprinkle with 2 tablespoons flour and 1 teaspoon dry mustard and cook a few minutes more. Add 8 cups stock and 1 teaspoon Vegemite. Bring to a boil, add 4 sprigs thyme and 1 bay leaf. Cover, and simmer for 20 minutes. For true French onion soup, serve with floating toasted cheese. **If you have it:** Add ¼ cup white wine and ⅓ cup fortified wine (e.g. brandy, sherry, port, madeira) or ½ cup red wine with the stock.

- **ONION AND BEETROOT CHUTNEY.** Goes everywhere tomato sauce goes and with a bright purple colour to boot. Steam 3–4 large beetroot until tender. Cool, peel and mash. Combine 6 chopped onions, ⅓ cup sugar, 1 teaspoon allspice and 1 cup red wine vinegar. Boil gently for 20 minutes. Add beetroot and reheat. Blend 1½ tablespoons plain flour with a second cup of vinegar and add to beetroot mixture. Stir over medium heat until the mixture boils and thickens. Makes 4 cups. **If you have it:** Sour cream or yoghurt creates a dip. Add 3 sprigs thyme with onions and discard before bottling.

- **ONION PAKORA.** Combine 1½ cups plain flour and 1 teaspoon each tumeric, garam masala, coriander powder and cumin. Add 1 cup water gradually to make a batter. Add 2 diced white or red onions and 1 grated carrot. Deep-fry spoonfuls of mixture in hot oil until deep golden colour. Serve with mango chutney and mint yoghurt sauce. **If you have it:** Replace flour with besan (chickpea flour).

- **SRI LANKAN COCONUT ONIONS.** For an unusual accompaniment to any curry. Sauté 3 chopped onions slowly in a little oil, for about 10 minutes, until they begin to brown. Add ¼ cup coconut milk, 1 tablespoon soy sauce, 1 tablespoon sugar, 1 teaspoon lemon/lime juice and ¼ teaspoon cinnamon, and simmer for 10 minutes. Serve over seafood or poultry. **If you have it:** Add steamed snow peas and carrots along with strips of chicken and you have a meal.

- **TOMATO HONEY ONIONS.** Combine 1 tablespoon melted butter with 4 tablespoons tomato sauce, 3 tablespoons honey and chilli to taste. Pour over 4 quartered onions and bake until soft. (Also works well in the microwave.) Serve with steak or lamb. Lovely on sandwiches. **If you have it:** If you like it hot, replace some of the honey with sweet chilli sauce.

Caramelised onion

A great solution to an onion glut. Heat 8 chopped onions in ⅓ cup oil. Cook very slowly for 15–20 minutes. Stir occasionally and add ¼ cup stock as needed to keep the mixture moist. Don't be tempted to turn the heat up, you don't want the onions to burn. When onions are softened and golden, add ⅓ cup sugar and ¼ cup balsamic vinegar. Cook over low heat for a further 5–10 minutes, stirring occasionally, until sticky and caramelised. Makes 2 cups. Keeps 3–4 days in the fridge and freezes for up to 3 months.

If you have it: In the final few minutes add a small splash of fortified wine, such as brandy, sherry, madeira, or port. Or a pinch of fresh thyme or finely chopped rosemary. Or 2 tablespoons grainy mustard. Or go with the chef's trick, a blob of butter to make it shine.

I caramelise onions fast over a hot flame on a barbecue. The secret is salt. It's an old Indian trick. With a good sprinkle of salt you can cook the cr*p out of them and they won't burn. Mike S

Caramelised Onion Ideas

- **BEER GRAVY.** Combine 1 cup each caramelised onions, beer and beef stock and 2 teaspoons Worcestershire sauce. Simmer for 20 minutes. Serve with all meat and poultry.
- **DIP.** Add 1 cup caramelised onion to 200 g tub plain yoghurt and 220 g tub cream cheese. Serve with vegetable sticks.
- **FAST ONION SOUP.** For every cup beef stock, add 2 tablespoons caramelised onions and 1 teaspoon Worcestershire sauce. **If you have it:** Add 1 teaspoon dry sherry. Top with stale bread and grated cheese. Heat under griller and voilà! French onion soup.

- **PASTA.** Fry 250 grams chopped bacon, 200 grams mushrooms, a couple of crushed cloves garlic. Add 1 cup caramelised onion. Toss through pasta with 100 grams goat's cheese.
- **PIE.** Pre-prepare a homemade base or follow instructions on packet. Fill with mixture of ½–¾ cup caramelised onions, 2 eggs, 1½ cups milk, 1½ cups cheese and a generous pinch of nutmeg. Bake in hot oven for 30 mins or until it sets and the top is golden.
- **PIZZA.** Scatter caramelised onions, just-cooked sweet potato/pumpkin slices and goat's cheese. **If you have it:** Top with finely chopped sage.
- **POTATO-MASHED/BAKED.** Stir through mashed potato. Scatter on top of baked potato with a dollop of sour cream.
- **RICE SALAD.** Combine 1 cup caramelised onion with 2 cups cooked rice and ¾ cup dried cranberries. Dress with 3 tablespoons oil and 1 tablespoon raspberry or rice vinegar. **If you have it:** Add 1 teaspoon orange zest and ½ cup pine nuts or chopped walnuts.
- **VINAIGRETTE.** Add 1–2 tablespoons caramelised onion to 2 tablespoons oil, 2 tablespoons lemon juice, 1 crushed clove garlic and 2 teaspoons coarse grain mustard. Dress everything from a leafy green salad, warm roasted root vegetables or a salad of tinned or fresh beans.

Orange

The juice on peel, pips and pith

Nothing beats a fresh orange. But what if you've bitten off more than you can eat with that jumbo bag, or they're proving to be less juicy or sweet than you hoped? Ideas here aplenty for the peel, the pulp and the juice.

The trick to making sure oranges are eaten up is to eat them without peeling. Slice them into pieces that fit perfectly in your mouth so you can bite the flesh away from the peel. My sister and I used to call them orange smiles. Still do.

Simon W

Fabulous flaws

Don't ditch those blemished ones. An orange that's been injured, such as a rub mark from a branch, is quite likely to be juicier than a perfect specimen. To heal itself, it has had to create more juice.

Buying

Variety	Qualities	Uses	Season
Navel	Seedless, thick skin, easy to peel	Eating fresh	April–October (a new variety is available as late as January)
Valencia	Smooth, thin skin	Juicing	September–April
Seville	Strong flavour, too bitter to eat uncooked	Marmalade Moroccan tagine dishes	Around July (hard to find)
Blood oranges (a type of Navel)	Sweet and juicy	Desserts, salads, marmalade	Short time around April

All varieties should feel firm and heavy for their size. But don't be misled by the size. The smaller the orange, the juicier it will be. Big ones dry out quicker.

For **Navels**, look at the 'button' on the stem end of the orange. If there is a nice, green cap, it's fresh. If the button is brown, and if the edges are turning up a bit, it could be getting old. This is such a good indicator that importers of Australian Navels use it to grade the fruit.

For **Valencias**, don't worry if the skin is green in late summer. That's nature's way of protecting the fruit from the sun. It's called re-greening. In fact, some consider the greener the skin, the sweeter and juicier the orange because it's proof that the fruit has been left on the tree until ripe and ready.

Storing

Whole: In a cool spot in the house if you're eating them daily. Otherwise keep loose in the fridge crisper drawer for up to two weeks, not in plastic bags. If you see a sunken spot on an orange or the rind starting to go white, that's sour rot which is highly contagious. Remove the offending specimen immediately!

Home-grown oranges dry out quickly so eat as soon as possible after picking.

Cut: Wrapped in plastic in the fridge.

Peel: Best to peel and grate rind as needed. Remember when you used to buy oranges wrapped in tissue? That was partly to stop them losing moisture. Now they're waxed, so wash before peeling and grating. The wax isn't dangerous, but hardly tasty.

Juice: **Valencia** juice keeps for 10 days in the fridge and loses very little of the Vitamin C (use sterilised bottles). With **Navels**, best to juice when you want it as the juice can get a bit bitter after a few hours exposure to air.

Freezing: Early **Valencias** are the best for freezing. Put juice in iceblock trays then store blocks in plastic container. Or freeze juice in plastic bottles (make sure to leave space for expansion) for up to 6 months.

Freeze wedges, children love them on a hot day.

Freeze peel in an airtight bag and you'll preserve those aromatic oils.

WASTE WARRIOR TIP

After you've squeezed your oranges, don't throw out those empty halves. Put one inside the other to save space and freeze to use peel later. Or what about using them as containers for fruit salad, sorbets and ice-cream? Maybe even savoury dishes with chicken or seafood? Scrape out membranes and loose pith. They keep for 4 days in the fridge.

ACID TEST

Don't brush your teeth within at least 30 minutes of eating citrus because you could actually brush part of your teeth away! Citrus softens the surface of teeth and rigorous brushing can scratch them.

Using

How much

1 orange = ⅔ cup puree
= 4 teaspoons grated rind
= ¼ cup juice
= ½ cup bite-sized pieces

Using Up

A Spare One or Two

- **BEETROOT BONUS.** Add pieces of orange to steamed and buttered carrots or beetroot.
- **BITTERSWEET SALAD.** Peel and thinly slice 3 oranges and 1 red onion. Toss with a handful of pitted olives in 1–2 teaspoons olive oil and a pinch coriander seeds. Store in fridge for a couple of hours before serving.
- **BROCCOLI SAUCE.** Sauté ½ cup chopped spring onions and 2 minced garlic cloves in 1 tablespoon each olive oil and butter. Combine ¾ cup orange juice, ½ cup dry white wine, 1 tablespoon grated orange rind, ½ teaspoon dry mustard. Add to onion mix and cook until thickens. Great with broccoli.
- **ORANGE AND LEMON SALAD.** Combine 3 sliced oranges, 6 finely sliced radishes and 4 grated carrots. Dress with ¼ cup each olive oil and lemon juice, flavoured with 1 teaspoon each cumin and cinnamon.
- **RELISH.** Sprinkle thick orange slices lightly with brown sugar and cinnamon, maybe top with a dab of butter and grill until mixture bubbles and orange pieces are tender. Serve with sausages and cold meats.
- **SANDWICH SPREAD.** Blend 1 orange, roughly chopped and seeded, ¼ cup raisins or sultanas and ¾ cup pecans.

Pithy hint

If you want peeled oranges minus the pith, put them in a hot oven for a few minutes before peeling, or cover with boiling water. Let stand for 5 minutes. The peel should just slide off. For recipes that use orange slices, removing the peel is a matter of taste. It's probably a good idea for oranges with very thick skins.

- **WHOLE ORANGE CAKE.** Boil 2 oranges for 40 minutes, completely submerged in water, until soft. Cool. Remove seeds and puree. Add 2½ cups almond meal and 1 teaspoon baking powder. Whisk 5 eggs and ¾ cup caster sugar for up to 10 minutes until light and fluffy. Fold in orange mixture. Bake in a moderate oven 40–45 minutes until light golden. Cover with foil and bake further 20–25 minutes. Serve with syrup: combine juice and zest 1 orange, 1¼ cups honey and 2 tablespoons water and simmer for a few minutes. **If you have it:** Add 2 teaspoons orange blossom water.

Juice

- **FRENCH TOAST/SCRAMBLED EGGS.** Use orange juice with egg instead of milk. Maybe some grated rind for extra flavour.
- **MUFFINS.** Dip a sugar cube (very briefly) in orange juice or orange syrup and pop in the top of each one before baking.
- **PANCAKES.** Substitute orange juice for the water, milk or buttermilk in the recipe.
- **PORRIDGE.** Use orange juice in place of some water in the cooking, or pour over cooked porridge.

JUICY HINT

Want to squeeze that last drop out of your oranges? Check out the Juicy hint on p. 150.

Peel

- **ASPARAGUS.** Fry breadcrumbs with grated orange for a great topping for asparagus. Stores for weeks in the freezer.
- **CAKES.** Great zesty flavour for icing, biscuit bases for cheesecakes, and in cake and muffin mixes.

- **PRUNES.** Add a strip of orange or mandarin peel to stewed prunes.
- **CHICKEN.** The orange rice and chicken dish (see p. 211) uses up the rind of two oranges.

Aroma tip

Dry the peel in the oven and pop into the water in your oil burner for a tangy aroma – or throw onto the open fire. In Ireland, they bake old oranges in the oven to dry them out and then hang them by the fire with a few cloves stuck into the fruit.

I'll drink to that

Hot chocolate. Dip in a strand or two. Chocolate and orange: always a winner.

Teapot. Add dried peel to your brew.

Bumper Harvest

- **JELLY.** Uses up a whopping 10 oranges. Boil ½ cup sugar in about 4 tablespoons water to make a syrup. Add the rind 2 oranges. Set aside. Juice all 10 oranges and strain through a sieve. Dissolve 2 tablespoons gelatine in some of the juice. Add this to the rest of the juice. Strain syrup and add to juice. Stir and put in fridge to set. For a Fancy touch, pour the jelly back into the orange halves. **If you have it:** Blood oranges are ideal. Replace 1 orange with a lemon.
- **MARMALADE.** No need to turn the kitchen into a major construction site. Just boil 1 kilogram whole oranges in water for 1 hour until soft, then remove oranges and reduce liquid to ⅓ cup. Peel oranges when cool. Discard pips. Finely shred about ¾ cup peel (after removing as much white pith as possible). Puree flesh and strain. Add puree and peel to

reduced liquid along with 2⅔ cups caster sugar. Bring to boil and cook, stirring frequently, until it reaches setting point. Fill sterilised jars. Makes about 3 cups.

- **SORBET.** Bring orange juice and sugar to the boil (around ¼ cup sugar for every 1 cup juice), stirring until sugar dissolves. Cool mixture before putting in the freezer. Whisk after an hour to break it up. At this point you could fold in a stiffly whisked eggwhite. Freeze for at least 30 minutes before serving. **If you have it:** Put a couple of star anise in at the beginning – remember to take them out before you cool the mixture.

- **SYRUP.** Reduce 4 cups orange juice over medium heat to about a quarter of the original amount. Add 1 cup sugar and zest from 2 oranges and simmer for a couple of minutes. Strain cooled syrup and store in sterilised bottle. Keeps for 3 months. Use syrup in desserts like ice-cream, for baking cakes, scones and bread, adding to salad dressings and making iced drinks.

Fancy touch

Try making an orange rose. Peel the orange in one continuous length and roll up tightly, skin side out, to form a rose. Hold it together by pushing a wooden tooth pick through it. Keep in fridge or freezer until needed. Garnish for any dish with orange as an ingredient.

Have a go

Crystallised Peel

This is time consuming and a bit fiddly. But when you get it right, it's worth it.

Ingredients

Orange peel (Save up all those squeezed cups until you have a big bagful in the freezer.)
White sugar
Caster sugar
Chocolate (for coating)

Method

Cut orange peel into neat strips and boil in water for 1 hour, changing the water every 20 minutes.

Scrape off all white pith (it's bitter).

Bring to the boil a mixture of 2 parts sugar to 1 part water and simmer peel in liquid until peel becomes translucent, the water reduces and the syrup thickens. (The trick is stop before the peel starts to stick together, as it's a job to separate them!)

Resist stirring during this process as this can cause the sugar to crystallise. If that happens, just boil it all up again and return to a simmer.

Spread peel out on greaseproof paper until dry.

(Save syrup for drinks and cakes.)

Roll peel in caster sugar.

For an extra touch, dip ends in melted chocolate.

If you end up with some short bits that break off, use in muffin and cake recipes or stuff into dried dates along with an almond, then dip in chocolate.

Potato

Reinvent everyone's favourite vegetable

Potatoes are gregarious, they seem to go with everything, and they keep for ages. So what's the problem? Maybe you're just in need of a little inspiration to use them up. What about pizza, curry or even German strudel cake?

During the war my mum, a newlywed, was required to make a meal for the men in the shearing shed. Trouble was the only ingredient was potatoes. After potato soup, the men had potato pancakes as a substitute for meat, mashed potatoes and roast potatoes. Her father-in-law was impressed. Pam M

Buying

Unwashed and brushed potatoes should last twice as long as washed. But be careful, it all depends on how long they've taken to get to you. There can even be a few green potatoes hiding under the dirt.

Chat or new potatoes should be eaten within a few days.

Cooking style	Variety
Mash	Coliban, Desiree, Dutch Cream
Boil, steam	Desiree, Pink Eye
Roast, bake	Coliban, King Edward, Pink Eye
Microwave	Nadine
Salad	Kipfler, Pink Eye
Soup, puree	Dutch Cream
Pizza, focaccia	Kipfler
Fry	Sebago
Any style	Sebago, Desiree, Golden Delight (Woolworth's variety) and Royal Blue

Storing

Whole: There's a bit of debate about storing in the fridge but we don't think it's a good idea. Best keep potatoes in a cool, dark, dry place – away from sources of heat and out of sunlight – to avoid greening and sprouting. Ideally, take them out of the plastic bag and put them in paper bags if you can or line their new home with paper towels. At the very least punch a few holes in the plastic bag. Potatoes breathe.

Washed potatoes keep up to a month, unwashed up to two.

Putting potatoes in your fridge can turn the starch to sugar, change the flavour and increase the glycaemic index (GI). But in the spirit of open debate we include:

> **The fridge is the place to store potatoes, especially washed potatoes. They green a lot faster out of the fridge. But even unwashed potatoes, we find they keep better in the fridge.** **Greengrocer**

Extreme Sport Cooking

No, you shouldn't eat green potatoes, even if you cut the green bits off. The fact that lots of people have done so and lived to tell the tale should in no way encourage you. The colour, by the way, is caused by exposure to light.

Cut: Peeled too many potatoes? Cover them with cold water and put in the fridge. If you like you can add a couple of drops of vinegar, 1 teaspoon lemon juice or pinch of sugar. (Just like flowers this will make them last longer.) They'll last up to four days if you do this, especially if you also change the water daily.

Freezing: Cooked potatoes don't freeze well. They become mushy when thawed. Ideally, freeze partially cooked potatoes and potato dishes. This doesn't seem to affect the texture. Then finish off the cooking when you're ready to eat them.

Cooked: You're better off trying to use up cooked potatoes in another dish than freezing them. Mind you, if you've got a dish where you won't notice a bit of mush, like soup, go for it.

Using

How much

3 medium potatoes = 450 grams
= 2½ cups raw diced or grated
= 2 cups mashed
= 2 cups salad
= 2 cups hot chips

Ideally, don't peel. Most of the good stuff is in the skin. Soak in water and use a scrubbing brush or a scouring pad. Trim away eyes or blemishes with a knife. At the very least, get slapdash with the peeler and leave great slabs still on – when else can you claim nutritional benefits for a half-hearted job? Certainly with small, new potatoes, a scourer is all you need. We include a recipe for peel itself for those of you who peel and then feel guilty.

Roast potatoes the Irish way (aka The Method).

1. Boil or steam the potatoes a little first – don't allow them to cook completely – then roast them.
2. When you put the potatoes in the baking dish, shake them up a little bit so their surface is roughened.

The result? Gorgeous crispy potatoes.

Using Up

Mash

- **COLCANNON.** An Irish staple and a Sunday night dinner winner. Melt 50 grams of butter, and fry a couple of sliced leeks until they start to soften. Add ½ sliced whole cabbage and ¼–½ cup milk, cover and steam until the cabbage is cooked. Stir in 4 cups mash and season well. **If you have it:** Chopped crispy bacon is great.

- **GERMAN POTATO CAKE.** Okay it's a lot of effort to use up a mashed spud, but it's a great cake and a terrific talking point. Add 1 tablespoon butter to ½ cup mash (1 largish potato). Add 1 small cup sugar, 1 beaten egg, 2 cups self-raising flour, ¾ cup milk, ½ cup sultanas and ½ teaspoon lemon essence or 1 teaspoon lemon zest. Put in 23 cm cake tin and layer with raw fruit of your choice, e.g. sliced apples, plums or cherries. Cover with crumble made from 1 cup plain flour, 1 cup sugar, 125 grams butter and ½ teaspoon nutmeg. Melt butter and combine. Bake in moderate oven for about 40 minutes.
- **PUFF.** Take 4 cups cooked potato, mash with 4 tablespoons butter and beat in 4 eggs and 1 cup milk. Baked in a hot oven for 20 minutes, it puffs up, just like the name says.
- **SCOTTISH BREKKIE SCONES.** Combine 1 cup cold mash to ½ cup flour and 3 tablespoons butter to form dough. Roll until 2–3 centimetres thick and cut into rounds. Fry in hot pan, 3–4 minutes each side or until brown.
- **SHEPHERD'S PIE.** Mashed potatoes can turn bolognaise sauce into shepherd's pie. Put meat sauce into casserole dish, top with mashed potato and bake. Dot with flecks of butter.
- **SKORDALIA.** A cold Greek potato and garlic dip. Lovely with bread. Great on vegies. Take 2 cups of mash and throw in blender with 6–8 cloves garlic, ½ cup olive oil and a couple of teaspoons of lemon juice until smooth.
- **SOUP.** Take a couple of cups of cooked potatoes, several bay leaves, 1 finely chopped onion and 2–3 cups milk (or cream). Throw the lot in a pan and cook on low heat for at least 30 minutes, so the herbs infuse into the liquid. Thin with water or stock. **If you have it:** Cook with thyme leaves and add chopped parsley just before serving.
- **VEGETABLE MASH.** If you've only got 1–2 potatoes, that doesn't mean you can't have mash. Just bulk it up with a little mashed carrot, sweet potato, pumpkin or celeriac. And while you're at it, don't stop at butter and milk, add garlic, finely chopped onions – fried until they are brown, English mustard or blue cheese.

WASTE WARRIOR TIP

Don't throw out those leftovers from the chippie. Try our hot potato chip frittata.

In a little oil, sauté any vegies you have handy – onion, capsicum, mushroom, zucchini. Add the cold chips and warm through. Add lightly beaten seasoned eggs and keep making holes in the mixture so that the egg can run through and cook. When nearly done, put the pan under the griller for a minute or two to brown. Great hot or cold.

Leftovers

- **TWICE BAKED.** Don't throw out leftover baked potatoes. Remove a thin slice from top of each and scoop out the middle, keeping the skins intact. Mash the pulp with flavourings and spoon back into skins. Sprinkle with shredded cheese. Bake in a moderate oven or until the cheese melts.
- **TWICE ROASTED.** You can re-roast potatoes. Dip in water and pop back in the oven for 20 minutes. Or chop up and put in a frittata or omelette.

PERFECT MASH

The big tip is not to let the potatoes get cold or they'll turn gluey. Return to pot on stove after cooking on very low heat. This will also dry them out, which is a good thing. Then add your milk, butter, cream, sour cream: whatever. Some cooks use a whisk or even an electric blender until the mash is creamy and fluffy.

The real aficionados cook the potatoes on salt in the oven to desiccate the vegetable. If you've gone to that much trouble, use white pepper to season so there are no 'unsightly' black pepper specks.

Peel

- **SEASONED.** Melt 1 tablespoon butter and use it to coat about 1 cup cleaned potato peels. Toss with dry seasoning, such as chicken salt or lemon pepper (or both). Bake in a moderately hot oven for about 15 minutes until crunchy.

A Glut of Potatoes

- **HASH BROWN.** How do just potatoes and oil taste so good? For maximum crispness, squeeze all the moisture you can out of grated potato before you fry. Season and press into hot, oiled frypan. It should be golden after 5–7 minutes. Flip and repeat.
- **PIZZA.** White pizza is as good as its red tomato cousin and you don't need cheese. Finely slice 4 potatoes, toss with ½ cup oil, 6–8 crushed cloves garlic and a couple of tablespoons finely chopped thyme, oregano and/or rosemary. Season well. Layer on 2 small pizza bases or 2 large slices flat bread and bake for 15 minutes until the potatoes are soft.
- **SEAFOOD SALAD.** Add fish to a potato salad for a more-ish meal. Combine 4–5 cooked cubed potatoes with around 300 grams flaked fish, cooked, canned or smoked. Add ½ bunch sliced spring onions. Dress with ⅓ cup olive oil and 2 tablespoons each creamed horseradish and lemon juice. **If you have it:** Add ¼ cup chopped parsley or 2 tablespoons tarragon. A dozen bite-sized tomatoes. 1–2 hard-boiled eggs. **Second helpings:** The next day, mash it up, add an egg and breadcrumbs and shallow fry as fish patties.

Have a go

Spicy Balti Curry

Potatoes are a staple in curries as they absorb all the lovely spices. But in this one, they take star billing.

Ingredients

½ teaspoon cumin
½ teaspoon fennel
½ teaspoon mustard seeds
½ teaspoon fenugreek seeds
3 cloves garlic, crushed
3 centimetre knob ginger, grated
3 curry leaves
2 onions, diced
6 potatoes, diced
1 tablespoon ground coriander
Chilli
1–2 cups stock
¼ cup fresh coriander, chopped, for serving

Method

Stir-fry cumin, fennel, mustard and fenugreek seeds with garlic, ginger and curry leaves until fragrant: about 1 minute.

Add onions and cook for a further 5 minutes or until the onions are transparent.

Add potatoes, ground coriander and chilli to taste and mix well.

Add stock and simmer, covered, for 10 minutes until the potatoes are just tender.

Remove the lid to reduce some of the liquid before serving.

Serve sprinkled with fresh coriander. **If you have it:** Add spinach, a tin of tomatoes or 1 cup frozen peas.

Pumpkin

Some heavy-duty ideas with a hefty flavour

It's a storage issue: not only can the raw vegetable take up precious space, it's easy to cook more than the family can eat at one sitting. Pumpkin scones are not the only solution.

Buying

Whole: Select one with a hard, thick skin that feels heavy for its size. If you get one with some stalk attached, all the better. It helps protect the inside from damp and insects.

Cut pieces: Check the seeds aren't slimy. Flesh should be bright yellow-orange.

Season: Australian pumpkins available all year.

Variety	Appearance	Uses
Butternut	Bell shape Smooth, creamy-brown skin	Make the most of its flavour and colour in soups
Golden Nugget	Small and round Deep-orange skin and golden flesh	Mild flavour Ideal for hollowing out, stuffing and baking
Jarrahdale	Large and grey Sweet, deep orange flesh A winter variety from Western Australia	Easy to cut and peel Good in curries and baked
Jap (also called Kent)	Ribbed, shiny, grey-green mottled skin Deep-yellow flesh	Sweet, nutty flavour Great mashed and in Mediterranean dishes
Queensland Blue	One of the biggest pumpkins Tough, grey, heavily ribbed skin	Powerful flavour Good in casseroles, stews and tagines

Storing

Whole: On its side, so moisture can't collect overnight around the stalk. That's what causes it to rot.

Pumpkin will keep for a couple of months in a cool, dark, well-ventilated place. Lining the shelf with newspaper may help to keep it dry but probably isn't necessary. Hard-skinned varieties (such as **Queensland Blue** and **Jarrahdale**) store better than soft-skinned varieties (such as **Jap** or **Butternut**).

If you've grown your own, it'll keep even longer if you first 'cure' it. Leave your pumpkin in a warm, dry, sunny spot for at least two weeks to harden the skin.

Cut: When you get it home, remove the seeds and cover in plastic wrap. Pumpkin keeps in the fridge for up to a week.

Freezing: Yes, but you have to cook it thoroughly first. Good in chunks and mashed. Keeps for up to three months.

Cooked: Dishes containing pumpkin keep for three to five days in an airtight container in the fridge.

IT'S A-PEELING

Hate peeling pumpkin? Wait until it's cooked and it's so much easier.

Pig food?

Pumpkin soup would surely make it onto the list of Top Ten typical Aussie dishes, but post-World War II it was snubbed by many European migrants as 'pig food'.

During the War, many people lived on little else for long periods, as it was easy to find and cheap. And that stigma is only now disappearing.

Using

How much

1 cup pumpkin puree = 250 grams peeled pumpkin
1 cup pumpkin pieces = 170 grams

Popping pumpkin seeds

Rinse off the stringy bits, soak for a few hours then dry overnight. Bake in a moderate oven for about 15 minutes or toast in a frypan. You can add a little oil and salt. Don't let them burn, so stir and check frequently. They'll pop and dance around like popcorn.

Using Up

A Few Pumpkin Pieces

- **CHICKPEA AND PUMPKIN DIP.** Mash together 2 cups cooked pumpkin, 400 g can chickpeas, 200 g tub natural yoghurt and 2 teaspoons curry powder.
- **ENVELOPES.** Cut frozen pastry sheets into 4. Spread thick pasta sauce or pesto in the centre and top with 4–5 cubes roasted or steamed pumpkin. Lift the corners into the centre and seal. Brush the top with a little milk or beaten egg. Bake in a moderate oven until golden.
- **LAKSA.** Combine 3 tablespoons laksa paste, 1 cup vegetable stock and 400 mL can coconut milk. Cook for 2–3 minutes. Add 1 cup steamed pumpkin cubes, juice 1 lime and 2 tablespoons fish sauce. Heat through. Pour over cooked noodles. Top with coriander leaves.
- **MEAT CASSEROLE.** Pop in chunks of cooked pumpkin at the last minute.
- **PASTA.** To cooked pasta, add 1 cup cooked pumpkin cubes, 1½ tablespoons roasted pine nuts, 2–3 rashers fried and crumbled bacon or prosciutto and basil leaves. Toss in dressing of equal quantities olive oil and balsamic vinegar plus ½ teaspoon Dijon mustard.
- **PIZZA.** Chop up cooked pieces to add flavour and colour to your pizza. Great with baby spinach (cooked or raw), red onion and ricotta or fetta cheese.
- **ROASTED.** Spruce up those spare raw pumpkin pieces with olive oil mixed with a little ground cardamom, ground cinnamon and seasoning. Bake in moderate oven for about 30 minutes or until cooked. **If you have it:** Serve topped with sour cream and a sprinkle of pine nuts. Alternatively, mix 2 teaspoons each honey and cumin seeds with the oil before basting.
- **SALAD.** Mix cooked pumpkin cubes with chunks of cooked beetroot, baby spinach and crumbled fetta. Dress with 3 tablespoons olive oil and 1 tablespoon red wine vinegar.

WASTE WARRIOR TIP

Eat the skins. Let's face it – anything that saves peeling is a bonus. Roast the seeds (pepitas) to add to cool salads or hot vegetables. There you are. Only the stringy bits leftover to throw in the compost bin.

If you have it: Replace spinach with rocket. Replace fetta with toasted pine nuts.

A Little Effort

- **FETTA FRITTATA.** Sauté 3 cups steamed butternut pumpkin in a little oil for 5 minutes until softish and golden brown. Add 2 coarsely chopped zucchini and cook for another couple of minutes. Whisk together 6 eggs, ½ cup thickened cream, 200 grams crumbled fetta, ¼ cup finely shredded fresh basil leaves and seasoning. Pour egg mixture over pumpkin mixture. Cook on low heat until almost set. Brown under the griller.
- **STRUDEL.** Thinly slice and sauté 3 leeks for about 20 minutes in a little oil until soft and golden. Prepare filo pastry as instructed on the packet, using 6 sheets. Spread leeks over half the pastry leaving a 5-centimetre border on 3 sides. Top with 3–4 cups steamed or roasted pumpkin pieces. Sprinkle over 120 grams crumbled goats cheese. Brush edges with butter, fold pastry sheets over and press edges firmly to seal. Cut some steam vents. Brush with any remaining butter and sprinkle with ½ teaspoon cumin seeds. Bake in hot oven for 15–20 minutes or until golden and crisp.
- **WONTONS.** Fill each wonton wrapper with 1 heaped teaspoon mashed roast pumpkin with some finely chopped spring onion and grated ginger. Lightly brush round the outside with cold water. Scrunch up into a pouch, squeezing to seal. Do not overfill. Fry for 2–3 minutes until golden or steam for about 15–20 minutes, making sure wontons don't touch each other. (A tip is to line steamer with non-stick baking paper with slits in it.) Serve with soy sauce.

More than a Few Pumpkin Pieces

- **CHUTNEY.** Great with Indian dishes. Combine 1 kilogram peeled and diced pumpkin, 2½ cups malt vinegar, 1 cup honey, 1 large chopped onion and 1 tablespoon salt. Gently heat until sugar has dissolved. Quickly bring to the boil and then reduce heat and simmer for about 30 minutes, until the mixture is thickened and the pumpkin pieces are tender. Cool for a few minutes before ladling into warm, sterilised jars. Best after storing for 1 month. Keep in fridge after opening.

Makes 2–3 cups. **If you have it:** Add ½ cup raisins or diced cooking apple, 1 tablespoon coriander seeds and 1 tablespoon grated ginger.

- **PANETTONE PUDDING.** Pumpkin and panettone together take bread and butter pudding to a new level. Follow the basic recipe (see p. 35) but reduce the milk to 1¼ cups and add ½ cup or more pureed pumpkin, ½ teaspoon ground cinnamon, a little grated fresh nutmeg and ½ teaspoon ground ginger. It's cooked when it's golden but still a bit wobbly.
- **PUMPKIN PIE.** Pre-prepare a homemade base or follow instructions on packet. Blend together 2 cups pumpkin puree, 2–3 eggs, 1½ cups thickened cream, 1 cup brown sugar and 2–3 teaspoons spices (mainly cinnamon plus some ground ginger, nutmeg, ground cloves or allspice) until smooth. Pour into pastry base. Bake in a moderate oven for 10–15 minutes and then in a slow oven for a further 30–40 minutes. The centre will still be a little soft, but will set as it cools. Serve cold with cream or ice-cream. **If you have it:** Sprinkle with sunflower seeds before baking.
- **RICE CAKES.** Sauté 1 chopped onion and 1 crushed clove garlic in butter. Add 2–3 cups pumpkin cut into small pieces, 1 cup rice and 2 cups vegetable stock. Bring to the boil, then reduce heat and simmer until rice absorbs the liquid. Stir ½ cup grated cheddar through rice mixture. Cool. Roll into balls, flatten slightly and fry until golden on both sides.
- **SCONES.** Cream 45 grams butter and 2 tablespoons sugar. Add 1½ cups mashed pumpkin, ½ cup milk, 1 egg, 2½ cups self-raising flour and ½ cup sultanas. Roll out onto floured surface and cut into scones. Bake in very hot oven for 12 minutes or until golden. Makes 16 scones.
- **SPICY SOUP.** Sauté 1 sliced leek and 1 crushed clove garlic in oil until soft. Add 1 finely chopped chilli to taste, ½ tablespoon grated ginger and 1½ teaspoons cumin seeds and stir for 1 minute or until fragrant. Stir in a couple of chopped carrots, about 1 kilogram chopped pumpkin and ⅓ cup yellow split peas. Add 4–5 cups stock, bring to the boil and simmer for about 1 hour until split peas are soft. Blend until smooth. Serve hot, topped with coriander.

Have a go

Vegetable Lasagne

Ingredients

2 onions, chopped
2 cloves garlic, crushed
2 zucchini, diced
1 beetroot, diced
300 g pumpkin, cut into chunks
2×400 g cans chopped tomatoes
2 heaped tablespoons tomato puree
2 cups vegetable stock
2 tablespoons butter
2 tablespoons flour
1 cup milk
¼ teaspoon nutmeg
½ cup Swiss cheese, grated
¼ cup parmesan, grated
450 g pre-cooked lasagne sheets
Extra grated cheese

Method

Sauté onions and garlic in a little oil.

Add zucchini, beetroot and pumpkin and cook for a few minutes.

Add tomatoes, tomato puree and enough stock to cover vegetables. Simmer for 10–15 minutes, adding more stock if necessary.

To make the cheese sauce, whisk butter, flour, milk and nutmeg continuously over a medium heat until the sauce begins to boil and thicken. Cook on very low heat for 2 minutes. Add cheeses. Season to taste.

Layer casserole dish with lasagne sheets and spoon half the vegetable mixture into casserole dish. Top with another layer of lasagne sheets and spread with half the cheese sauce. Repeat, finishing with cheese sauce. Sprinkle with extra grated cheese.

Bake in a moderate oven for about 30 minutes, until golden brown.

Why you should handle with care

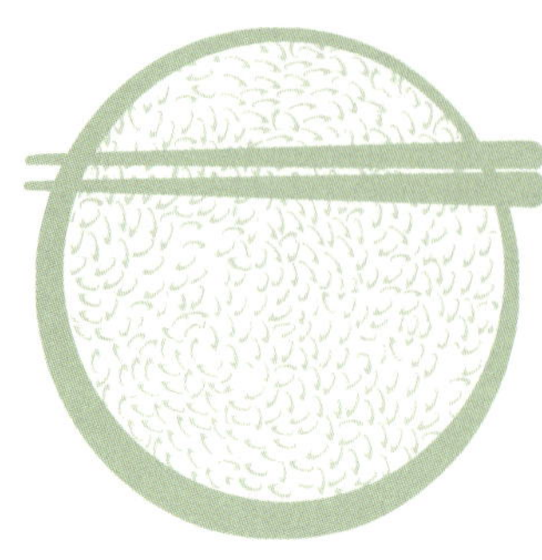

Who hasn't cooked too much rice at some stage? It's so easy to let it go to waste. No need. There are many sweet and savoury ways to use a spare spoonful, cupful or potful.

It's not the traditional rice pudding my gran used to make, but it's still perfect comfort food. Mix leftover rice with some milk, an egg, some raisins, a bit of cinnamon, and a bit of sugar and bake until it sets. I like it hot. And cold.

Jenny W

Dangerous rice

Did you know that cooked rice is a significant cause of food poisoning? But you can't really blame the rice – it's no more dangerous than cooked meat and chicken. The problem lies in our attitude towards it. We're just too laid back. Remember to get it into the fridge fast. (Check out the 2–4 hour rule on p. 158.)

Buying

Variety	Texture	Uses
Long	Firm and fluffy Grains stay separate	The flavours of jasmine and basmati complement savoury dishes, especially Asian dishes like fried rice, stir-fries, red and green curries
Medium	When you want both fluffiness and a little stickiness A slightly clingy, creamy texture	Arborio is a popular choice for risotto, paella, dolmades, soup, casseroles, creamed rice and desserts
Short	Sticky	For sushi and most Japanese and Korean dishes
Brown	Slightly chewy Outer bran layer is the reason it takes longer to cook	Nutty flavour for poultry stuffing, rissoles, savoury stuffed capsicums and soup

Storing

Uncooked: Keep dry, preferably in a cool dark place. White rice keeps indefinitely, but brown rice needs to be used within about six months.

Cooked: Cool quickly and store in the fridge. (See the 2–4 hour rule on p. 158.) Adding a little water before storing will make your rice moist when you reheat it. Keep it in fridge for only one day and only reheat once.

Freezing: Cooked rice keeps for up to 1 month.

Using

How much

Child portion = about 2 tablespoons uncooked rice
Adult portion = about ½ cup
4 adult portions = 2 cups

Find your rice is too sticky? Try rinsing before cooking – it gets rid of a lot of the starch. The rice will taste better too.

When you're in a hurry, soak the rice in cold water until you're ready to start cooking. (Drain before cooking in fresh water.) It speeds up the cooking time, as well as getting rid of that starch.

DID YOU KNOW?

Brown rice has a shorter shelf life because of the outer layer of bran. Those healthy oils, unfortunately, can turn the rice rancid.

Using Up

A Cupful or Less

- **CABBAGE ROLLS.** Boil cabbage leaves, a few at a time, until limp. Drain. Sauté 1 chopped onion in a little oil for a couple of minutes. Add 1 crushed clove garlic and continue cooking until onion is soft. Add 250 grams minced lamb, ¾ cup cooked rice, 1 egg and 1 teaspoon Worcestershire sauce. Place tablespoon of filling on cabbage leaf and roll into a sausage shape, tucking in sides to contain filling. Pack rolls closely together in baking dish. Pour over thick tomato sauce. Bake in moderate oven about 40 minutes until rolls are tender.
- **HAM ROLLS.** Combine 1 cup cooked rice with 1 tablespoon mayonnaise and 2 teaspoons mustard pickle. Spread rice mixture on thin slices of ham and roll up.
- **RISOTTO BALLS.** Shape cold risotto into balls, then press a cube of mozzarella into each one, making sure it's covered. Roll each ball in beaten egg and then grated parmesan. Set for ½ hour in fridge. Fry in hot oil until golden and serve immediately. Alternatively, combine risotto with crumbled fetta, shape into balls or cakes and fry.
- **SAVOURY FRUIT AND NUT SALAD.** Chop up a few snow peas, ½ small red onion, ½ capsicum and 1 apple. Mix through 1 cup cooked rice. Sprinkle in a few raisins and walnuts. Pour over dressing of 1 tablespoon red wine vinegar, ¼ cup olive oil, ½ teaspoon curry powder and a pinch brown sugar.
- **SOUP.** Add body with a couple of spoonfuls of cooked rice.
- **STUFFED CAPSICUM.** Sauté 1 chopped onion in a little oil for a couple of minutes. Add 1 crushed clove garlic plus chopped up Mediterranean vegies you have on hand, such as artichokes, roast capsicum, sun-dried tomatoes, zucchini or eggplant. Mix in 1 cup cooked rice, season and continue cooking until the mixture is fairly dry. Cut tops off 1–2 capsicum and take out the membrane and seeds. Stuff mixture into the capsicum, sprinkle with a little parmesan or fetta and

replace lid. Brush capsicum with oil or cover with homemade tomato sauce (see p. 218). Bake in a medium-high oven for 20–30 minutes until the capsicum shell is tender.

- **SUSHI ROLLS.** Not for the purists. Leftover short or medium grain is best to avoid everything from falling apart, and use a little mayonnaise to help bind the rice together. Spread a thin layer of rice on nori sheet (dried seaweed). Add a strip of filling along the centre – try avocado and tuna; grated carrot and cucumber; chopped chicken dipped in satay sauce. Roll up and cut to size. **If you have it:** Use wasabi or horseradish cream instead of mayonnaise. A bamboo sushi mat for rolling makes life easier.

The highs and the lows

Ever wondered why you sometimes seem to feel hungry quicker after eating Asian food? It could be because of the rice. The glycemic index (GI) affects our blood sugar levels. A high GI and our sugar levels shoot up and plummet down quickly. We want to eat again sooner. The GI of rice varies according to variety, but they're all pretty high. General rule is that the longer the rice grain, the lower the GI; and the stickier the rice, the higher the GI. Basmati has a higher GI than jasmine, while sushi rice is higher still.

Make a Meal of It

- **CHICKEN LIVER PILAFF.** Cook 4 rashers chopped bacon. Add 1 large chopped onion and sauté for 1 minute before adding 2 crushed cloves garlic. Continue cooking until onion is light brown. Add 200 grams chopped chicken livers and cook through (about 2–3 minutes). Add 125 grams sliced mushrooms which have been marinating for at least 1 hour in ½ cup olive oil, ¼ cup red wine vinegar and ⅓ cup chopped flat leaf parsley. Lightly combine 3 cups cooked rice with chicken liver mixture and 2 tablespoons toasted pine nuts. Season to taste. Dot with butter and bake in slow oven for 20 minutes.

- **FRIED RICE.** The trick is to use day-old rice (safely stored, of course) and not to treat the dish as the solution for every single morsel lurking in the fridge. Simple does it. First make a thin omelette with 4 eggs and cut it into strips. Stir-fry 3-centimetre knob grated ginger, 1 chopped onion for 2 minutes. Add 1 crushed clove garlic and 2 rashers chopped bacon or Chinese sausage and stir-fry for a further minute, or until lightly browned. Add 2 cups cooked rice and omelette strips along with 2–3 tablespoons oyster sauce and/or soy sauce and 2 chopped spring onions. Garnish with some coriander or crushed peanuts.
- **KEDGEREE.** Sauté ½ finely chopped brown onion in 1 tablespoon butter for 1 minute. Add 1 crushed clove garlic, 2-centimetre knob grated ginger and 1 tablespoon mild curry and continue cooking until onion is soft. Add equal amounts of cooked rice and cooked flaked fish – smoked is best – and heat through. Add two chopped lightly boiled eggs, handful of parsley and liquid (if you've poached the fish, use some of that). Heat through. Serve with chutney. **If you have it:** Add chilli, a couple of anchovies, ¼–½ cup frozen peas.
- **MEAT LOAF.** Sauté 1 finely chopped onion in a little oil until soft. Add 750 grams mince and thoroughly brown. Add 3 cups cooked rice, 2 crushed cloves garlic, 2 teaspoons allspice and 2 tablespoons or more fresh thyme or basil. Mix thoroughly and add ⅓ cup stock (less, if the rice is moist), 1 egg and 2 tablespoons Worcestershire sauce. Season to taste. Bake in a hot oven for about 20 minutes.
- **SWEET RICE FRITTERS.** For every cup of cooked rice, you will need 1 egg, 2 tablespoons self-raising flour, 1 tablespoon sugar and ⅓ cup milk. Make a batter with the flour, beaten egg and milk. Add sugar and rice. Fry heaped tablespoonfuls each side until golden and puffed. Drain on paper towels. Drizzle with honey, sprinkle with cinnamon or squeeze over some lemon juice. **If you have it:** Add raisins or sultanas, pine nuts or slivered almonds to the batter.
- **VANILLA RICE.** Beat together ½ cup coconut cream, ½–1 teaspoon vanilla, 300 mL carton cream (or half milk, half cream) and 3 tablespoons caster sugar until soft peaks form. Fold through about 2 cups cooked rice that's been chilled in the fridge. Serve with fruit.

Have a go

Orange Rice and Chicken

When the pantry's looking bare, this is a surprisingly tasty meal.

Ingredients

1 kg chicken breasts, quartered
¼ cup oil
1 onion, chopped
1 tablespoon grated fresh ginger (or 1 teaspoon powdered)
1 cup stock (if using cubes or powder, double the strength)
Rind 2 oranges, shredded
1 cup sugar
4 cups cooked rice
Salt and pepper

Method

Brown chicken pieces in oil. Remove.

Sauté onion in a little oil with ginger until soft. Add stock and stir. Return chicken and stir to make sure you get all the tasty brown bits from the bottom of the pan. Cook for 30 minutes.

Boil orange shreds in 2 cups water for 5 minutes. Drain and rinse.

Dissolve sugar in 1 cup water, add orange peel and boil gently until syrup thickens (about 10 minutes). Strain syrup over cooked rice, reserving peel.

Spread half the rice in an ovenproof dish. Top with chicken and onion mixture, half cooking liquid and half shredded peel. Top with rest of the rice and pour over rest of the liquid. Cover and cook in a slow oven for 40 minutes or until chicken is cooked through. Season to taste.

Squishy squashy surprises

Does everyone's fridge contain half a wizened tomato? You can also get stuck with that bulk buy that wasn't a bargain, or half a punnet that isn't as sweet as promised. But don't stop at Italian sauce, try Thai rice or Ethiopian chicken. There's even a recipe for spicy tomato cake at the end. It is a fruit after all.

Blow into your plastic bag of tomatoes and tie them up after you've bought them; it stops your vegies getting crushed on the way home. Amanda P

Buying

Evil tomatoes

Only 150 years ago, tomatoes were considered poisonous. Some cookbooks advised people to boil them for several hours – for safety's sake. Today, there are websites that denounce them as evil. And we don't think they're all kidding. The argument revolves around the fact that tomatoes belong to the same botanical family as the poisonous deadly nightshade. So do potatoes and capsicum: but they somehow escape the label, 'Spawn of Satan'.

HANDY HINT

The sniff test is a great way to choose tomatoes. Smell the stem end; ripe tomatoes have a full, fruity aroma.

Red is good, green is fine, but pink is suspect. That's because pink ones don't ripen very well but green patches will. Tomatoes should feel heavy for their size and give just a little when you squeeze them.

Season: All year, but they're at their best in summer. Most supermarket tomatoes are grown in Queensland, particularly those sold in Brisbane, Sydney and Melbourne.

Storing

Whole: At room temperature with the stem side up. (The area around the stem is the softest part of the tomato and the most easily bruised.) Refrigerated tomatoes won't ripen and tend to taste mealy. However, in hot weather or if your tomatoes get too ripe, you can pop them in the fridge for a few days to make them last longer. Take them out an hour before using for the best flavour.

Cut: Covered in the fridge, tomatoes keep a few days.

Freezing: You can throw tomatoes straight into the freezer, no need to cook. (Wrap or cover first.) Frozen fresh tomatoes are a clever alternative to canned. They turn to mush, but they're great for sauces, soups or stews. It's up to you whether you want to core and remove the skins first.

Cooked: Tomato dishes last a few days, covered, in the fridge and freeze well.

MYTHBUSTER

Sunlight doesn't ripen tomatoes; it's warmth. But if that warm spot isn't ripening them fast enough, put tomatoes in a paper bag with a banana or an apple. Thanks to the naturally occurring ripening gas, ethylene, you'll have ripe tomatoes in days. In general, tomatoes keep about a week.

How much

1 medium tomato = 125 grams
= ½ cup chopped

To peel fresh tomatoes, drop whole into boiling water for about 20 seconds. Remove and run under cold water. The skin should now slip off quite easily. It helps to make small incisions around the stem before you boil – like a cross – to give you a starting point when you peel.

If you don't have enough tomatoes for a recipe, make up the difference with tinned, or vice versa.

Using Up

A Sad Half

- **BREADCRUMBS.** Chop up and mix with breadcrumbs and melted butter. Sprinkle over just-cooked cauliflower.
- **DIP.** Add the pulp to cream cheese, along with fresh herbs for a refreshing dip or sandwich filling.
- **LENTILS.** Add to Indian dahl.
- **MUFFINS, CAKES AND PANCAKES.** Remove the skin, chop and replace some of the fruit in any baked recipe, like apple muffins or even blueberry pancakes. The flavour is swamped by the other fruit.
- **RISOTTO.** Add colour to risotto by sautéing chopped tomato just after the onion.
- **ROAST.** Slice and use to cover parts of a roast likely to dry out, e.g. breast of chicken or turkey. Or just pop in with roast vegetables, like onions, potatoes and carrots.
- **SOUP/STEW/PASTA SAUCE.** Chop and throw in while cooking or reheating – even when the original doesn't contain tomato.
- **STEAMED/BAKED FISH.** Add a sliced tomato when you're steaming fish fillets inside foil packages. (Along with sliced onion and herbs.)
- **STEWED FRUIT.** Tomatoes are a fruit. You can add them to stewed stone fruit or even apple sauce for extra bulk without affecting the flavour.
- **STIR-FRY.** Chop and mix with fresh coriander to sprinkle over each serve.

Just a Little Effort

- **CORN SALSA.** Chop up tomato and basil. Add cooked sweetcorn. Drizzle with olive oil. Serve with chicken or fish.

- **FRIED.** Not just for green tomatoes but firm red ones too. Dip fat slices in beaten egg mixed with a little water. Drain and coat with mashed cornflakes and sesame seeds. Pan-fry in butter and oil until golden on both sides.
- **MUSHROOMS.** Sauté mushrooms in a little butter. Add chopped tomatoes and tarragon. Serve on toast.
- **PASTA ZUCCHINI.** Chop up tomato with steamed zucchini and chopped oregano and basil. Stir through pasta with parmesan.
- **STUFFED.** Chop the tops off 4 medium tomatoes and scoop out the middle. Add a couple of tablespoons of pulp to 125 g cream cheese, with a dash of Tabasco and garlic chives. Stuff mixture back into tomatoes. **If you have it:** It's fiddly, but stuffed cherry tomatoes are an impressive party or picnic snack.
- **THAI RICE.** Sauté 1 chopped onion and 1 crushed clove garlic in a little oil. Add 3 chopped tomatoes, a couple of teaspoons of lemon juice and a couple of tablespoons of soy and sugar. Add 1 cup each rice, coconut milk and stock and bring to the boil. Reduce the heat and simmer until the liquid boils off.

Homemade 'sun-dried'

Sprinkle halved tomatoes with a mixture of half caster sugar and half salt. Cook cut side up on a baking sheet and on a low heat in the oven for two-and-a-half hours, or longer if you like them even more concentrated. Store in the fridge for a week.

Too Many Soft Tomatoes

- **CHUTNEY.** Works just as well with sausages as it does in sandwiches. Take 3 or 4 tomatoes, 1 chopped onion, 1 crushed clove garlic, 1 chopped apple, a couple of cloves, ½ teaspoon allspice and ¾ cup sugar. Simmer for 30 minutes, stirring occasionally. Add 2½ cups malt vinegar and cook for another half hour or until thickened. Keeps for a few weeks in fridge. Makes 1 cup.

- **GAZPACHO.** Puree 1 continental cucumber, 2 red capsicum, 1 red onion, 1 clove garlic and 6–7 tomatoes. Whisk in 1 cup breadcrumbs (2 slices bread), 1 teaspoon Worcestershire sauce and 1 tablespoon olive oil. Add sugar and Tabasco to taste. Chill.
- **SALSA.** Combine 4 chopped tomatoes, ½ finely diced red onion, ½ cup coriander, 1 tablespoon olive oil and 1 tablespoon lime or lemon juice. Add fresh chilli to taste. Serve with corn chips, or any meat or seafood. Makes about 2 cups. (See p. 148 for lemony version.)

Tomato sauce.

Sauté 2 crushed cloves garlic in a little oil until it starts to colour. Add 4–5 diced tomatoes. When you season, add sugar to taste. Stir until it thickens, about ½ hour. Add to pasta or pizza with parmesan and basil or try:

- **PATATAS BRAVAS.** Potatoes in a spicy tomato sauce. Roast bite-sized cubes of potatoes until golden. Heat homemade tomato sauce with a pinch of paprika and/or chilli. Spoon over the potatoes.
- **BEANS.** Slow cook green beans in garlicky tomato sauce with a pinch of allspice or cinnamon.
- **EGGS.** A popular African breakfast dish. Thicken sauce with chopped capsicum or mushrooms and form indentations in the mixture. Drop an egg into each. Cover. It's ready when the eggs are cooked to your liking.
- **FISH.** Add olives, capers and a bay leaf to the sauce and simmer fish fillets in the mixture until cooked.
- **PRAWNS.** Add ½ cup white wine or vermouth to 1 cup tomato sauce. Simmer 12 green prawns in the mixture for 1 minute, or until cooked. Toss through pasta and serve with chopped spring onions.
- **SPANISH CHICKEN.** Puree 12 hazelnuts with 1 cup tomato sauce. Pour over cooked chicken.

Have a go

Ethiopian Peanut Chicken

The dish thickens nicely with the peanut paste but you don't lose that flavour of fresh tomatoes.

Ingredients

4 pieces chicken
Large knob fresh ginger, grated
1 tablespoon tomato paste
1 tablespoon cooking oil
1 onion, well chopped
3 cups tomatoes, chopped
Sugar
½ cup peanut paste
Chilli to taste
2 cups eggplant or potato or carrot, peeled and cubed
Some chopped spinach
½ cup basil, chopped

Method

Boil chicken with ginger in about 2 cups water for 10 minutes. Set aside.

Fry tomato paste and onions in oil until the onions are clear.

Add tomatoes and sugar to taste.

Add the partially cooked chicken pieces, along with about half the water, to the tomato mixture.

Add peanut paste and chilli. Cook for 5 minutes.

Stir in vegetables and continue cooking until they are tender. Add more water as needed.

Add basil just before serving. Great with rice.

Spiced Tomato Cake

Hey, you have no problem making a cake from carrots. Why not tomatoes? It has a lovely spicy flavour.

Ingredients

1 cup dark brown sugar
1 cup mild-tasting cooking oil
3 eggs
3 cups SR flour
1 teaspoon nutmeg
1 teaspoon cinnamon
½ teaspoon salt
2 cups fresh ripe tomatoes, peeled, seeded and chopped
1 cup walnuts or pecans, chopped
1 cup dates or raisins, chopped

Method

Cream sugar and oil.

Add eggs one at time.

Add sifted dry ingredients, mixing well.

Stir in tomatoes, nuts, and dates or raisins.

Pour into cake tin and bake in preheated moderate oven for 45 minutes, or until cake tests done.

Cream Cheese Frosting

225 g tub cream cheese
Approximately 2 cups icing sugar

Beat together the cream cheese and icing sugar a little at a time, until the mixture is the consistency you desire.

Zucchini

Feed the family from starter to dessert

There are countless ways to serve zucchini (also called courgette). Just as well, really. If you decide to plant zucchini in your garden, it does have a tendency to go berserk and provide enough to feed an army.

> **Zucchini soaks up and improves the flavours of everything it's cooked with. Some say it's tasteless. I say it's genius.**
>
> **Neil C**

Buying

They come in different colours, from dark green (the most common) to light green, and yellow to cream, so mix 'n' match to make your meals look good.

The Lebanese variety is a greeny-grey colour and has a slightly nutty flavour. Be gentle with the yellow ones as they're a little more fragile than the others.

Flowers: The female flowers have a tiny zucchini attached – perfect as an edible handle. The male flowers are bigger – but have no zucchini attached.

Season: Available all year, but most prolific in summer and autumn as they don't like the cold.

Storing

Whole: We know that many of you store it in the fridge, but if you've noticed sunken pits on the skin of your zucchini, that's because it doesn't like being chilled. If you insist, use a plastic bag or leave them loose in the vegetable crisper. Zucchini keeps three to five days.

Cut: If you're ploughing your way through a giant specimen from the garden, just wrap the cut end in plastic. It will last a couple of days until you regain the will to have a go at another recipe.

Flowers: The flowers are delicate. Remove stamens/pistils in the centre and keep flowers open by inserting one into each other. Best advice is to use straightaway or store in fridge and use as soon as you can.

Freezing: Thank goodness you can easily freeze zucchini when you've finally had enough of that bumper crop. Just top, tail and wrap up. It'll be soft and you'll find liquid in the bag when you thaw it. Don't worry. Use it all in dishes like curries and soups.

Cooked: Keeps for a day in the fridge, but really only good for mushing up to add to stews and casseroles. Most cooked meals with zucchini – stir-fry, slices and soups – freeze beautifully.

Using

How much

1 medium zucchini = 20 centimetres
= 180 grams
= 1 cup grated

Salted water can burn the zucchini skin. If you love your salt, do it after cooking.

Using Up

One Sad Zucchini

- **FRIED RICE.** Dice finely and pop into mixture just before serving.
- **FRITTATA.** Grate into any egg dish – omelette, frittata, quiche – for colour and bulk without affecting flavour.
- **LASAGNE.** Add to vegetable or meat lasagne. In fact, any pasta dish.
- **PANCAKES.** Grate into pancake mix with a little grated parmesan.

- **SAUCE.** Chop into small pieces and cook in a little oil until it all melts into a sauce to pour over vegies.
- **SOUP, STEW, SAUCE, CURRY.** Mash up and add for extra body, to absorb those flavours.
- **STIR-FRY.** Pop julienne sticks in at the last minute.
- **THAI-STYLE SALAD.** Use a vegetable peeler to make fine ribbons. Use raw (or blanch very quickly, rinse under cold water and pat dry) and toss with bean sprouts and grated carrot in a Thai-style dressing of 1 tablespoon each fish sauce and sugar and ⅓ cup each oil and lime juice.

Bumper Crop

WASTE WARRIOR TIP

No need to peel zucchini. But if the recipe calls for it, or you need to scoop out the centre, freeze that peel and pop in the next soup, stew or sauce you make

- **RATATOUILLE.** Purists may scoff, but we reckon this one-pot version is the way to go. Sauté 1 large chopped onion and 1–2 crushed cloves garlic in a little oil. Add 1 red and 1 green capsicum, 4 tomatoes, 4 zucchini, all chopped. Cook slowly for 1–2 hours on the cooktop, depending on how chunky you want it. Add sugar to taste. **If you have it:** Add ¼ cup flat leaf parsley, ¼ cup basil and a pinch of thyme Add a dollop of tomato paste if tomatoes are not tasty enough.
- **ZUCCHINI AND BASIL SOUP.** It's incredibly green yet kids love it. Sauté 1 chopped onion and 2 crushed cloves garlic in a little oil. Add 6 roughly chopped zucchini, 3 cups stock, 2 teaspoons sugar and 1 tablespoon lemon juice. Simmer until zucchini is soft. Stir in 1 cup chopped basil and blend. Reheat and serve. Add a blob of plain yoghurt or sour cream, a sprinkle of paprika, and extra basil on top.
- **ZUCCHINI CURRY.** Zucchini goes in any curry but it gets top billing in this one. Sauté 1 diced onion, 1 large crushed clove garlic and ½ tablespoon grated ginger in a little oil. Add 1 teaspoon each ground coriander, garam masala and turmeric and ½ teaspoon each cumin and curry powder. Cook until fragrant. Add 3 sliced zucchini and 10 quartered mushrooms for a few minutes and mix until everything is coated. Add 400 g can tomatoes, cover and simmer until all ingredients are soft but not disintegrated. **If you have it:** Replace your cooking oil with ghee for an authentic Indian curry.

- **ZUCCHINI SLICE.** Whisk 1 cup self-raising flour with 5 eggs. Add 4 cups grated zucchini, 1 finely chopped onion, 1 cup grated cheese and ¼ cup vegetable oil. Bake in a pan (about 20 cm x 30 cm) in a moderate oven for about 30 minutes, or until cooked through. Great hot or cold. **If you have it:** Add a handful of chopped bacon, 1 grated carrot for colour or a layer of tomato through the middle.

A Little Effort

- **ZUCCHINI CHIPS.** Mix seasoned breadcrumbs with paprika. Coat zucchini sticks with yoghurt, then press into crumb mixture. Bake in a hot to very hot oven for 15–25 minutes, until golden brown.
- **ZUCCHINI PICKLE.** Accompanies cold meats and cheese. Cover 5–6 zucchini and 2 finely sliced onions in ¼ cup salt and leave overnight. Strain. Boil 2 cups white vinegar, 1 cup white sugar, 2 teaspoons each mustard seeds and turmeric and 1 teaspoon celery seeds for 2 minutes. Pour over zucchini mix and leave for 2 hours. Finally, simmer for a few minutes, making sure zucchini stays firm. Cool, then bottle. Makes 2–3 cups.

HANDY HINT

The flowers can be frozen too – insert one into another to keep them open a little and leave some air in the bag.

Overgrown Solutions

When you've turned your back and those cute little zucchini in the garden have turned into monster marrows.

- **BBQ.** Slice thin rounds, drizzle with olive oil and cook until soft. An alternative to eggplant or potato.
- **MEDALLIONS.** Slice into thick medallions and scoop out most of the fluffy centre, leaving a 'floor' to make individual serves. Try this rice filling: sauté 10–15 sliced mushrooms, a handful of pitted green olives and about ⅓ cup chopped spring onions in a little oil. Add 1 cup rice and 2 cups chicken stock. Boil and simmer until rice is soft. Add as much of the zucchini flesh as you like. Pop into the centres and bake until zucchini softens.
- **STUFFED ZUCCHINI.** Slice lengthwise down the middle. Scoop out the insides. Try this: sauté finely chopped onion and 1 crushed clove garlic in a little oil. Add 500 grams

minced lamb and brown. Add 1 teaspoon each ground cumin and ground coriander seeds, ½ teaspoon ground cinnamon, 1 tablespoon tomato purée and 1 cup seasoned stock. Add as much of the zucchini flesh as you like. Cook until most of the liquid has gone. Pile the lot back into the cavity, put the two halves together, secure with kitchen string and bake in a moderate oven about 30 minutes until zucchini is softish and centre is piping hot. Slice and serve.

- **ZUCCHINI BOATS.** Use large (but not humungous) ones as edible containers. Slice the tops off lengthwise, scoop out the centre, fill and bake until soft. Try this filling: combine 2 cups cold meats like salami and prosciutto with 1 cup chopped mozzarella, a handful of halved cherry tomatoes and ¼ cup parmesan.
- **ZUCCHINI PARMIGIANA.** Slice into thick rounds, coat in breadcrumbs or flour if you like, and bake for about 10 minutes. Cover slices with your favourite pasta sauce (try marinara), then top with parmesan and mozzarella and bake for another 15 minutes. Freezes for up to a month. **Second helpings:** Blend the lot to make a sauce for pasta or pour over vegies.

Flowers

If you want to impress, here's some flower power.

- Stuffed and roasted. Try a mixture of 1 cup ricotta cheese, ⅓ cup reggiano and some finely chopped basil. Makes enough for 18 flowers. Bake in moderately hot oven about 15 minutes. Or you could dip stuffed flowers in a beer batter (½ cup beer, ½ cup flour) and fry. Turn once. Takes about 3 minutes.
- Zucchini flower and tomato salad. Use your fingertips to remove stamens/pistils in centre of each flower. Plunge into pot of boiling water, then into iced water and drain. Chop 3 tomatoes into wedges, crumble 100 grams stilton cheese and thinly slice one pear. Toss the lot in olive oil and serve immediately.

Have a go

Choc-chip zucchini muffins

You can always say the green bits are pistachios if there are queries from the vegetably-averse family members!

Ingredients

3 eggs
1 cup vegetable oil
1¾ cups sugar
2 cups grated zucchini
2 teaspoons vanilla essence
3 cups self-raising flour
3 teaspoons cinnamon
1 cup choc chips

Icing

½ cup cream cheese
¼ cup sifted icing sugar
1 teaspoon lemon/orange rind
1 teaspoon lemon/orange juice

Method

Combine eggs, vegetable oil, sugar, grated zucchini and vanilla essence.

In another container, combine flour, cinnamon and choc chips.

Stir into egg mixture.

Spoon into muffin tray and bake in moderate oven for 20–25 minutes.

Meanwhile make the cream cheese icing: combine cream cheese, sifted icing sugar, lemon/orange rind and lemon/orange juice until smooth.

Acknowledgments

We would like to thank friends, family and workmates for not only eating our experiments but also testing out many tips for us; especially those of you who graciously indulged our obsessions about various foodstuffs as we worked through the chapters.

We're also grateful to all the organisations, farmers, growers and cooks as well as the food experts (official and otherwise) for their support, advice, tips and recipes.

Special thanks to Michael Bollen at Wakefield Press for taking us on and not trying to change us, and Julia Beaven for her patient and thoughtful editing and for guiding us through this process called publishing.

Wakefield Press is an independent publishing and distribution company based in Adelaide, South Australia.
We love good stories and publish beautiful books.
To see our full range of titles, please visit our website at www.wakefieldpress.com.au.